THE TRUE CHURCH (EKKLESIA)

The Undisputed Government
of Heaven on Earth

ANTHONY MWANGI

Crony Trading LTD

To the Lamb,
the King whose government cannot be challenged,
whose Word cannot be overturned,
and whose rest cannot be invaded.

To the Holy Spirit,
the Fire who builds the Bride,
the Breath who forms the Ekklesia,
the Sabbath who crowns the sons of light.

To Zion,
the dwelling place of God in His people,
the courtroom of mercy and justice,
the throne where heaven and earth become one.

And to every son, daughter, and seeker
who dares to rise into their true identity —
may this scroll ignite your fire,
steady your steps,
and usher you into the government
you were born to carry.

"Thy kingdom come.
Thy will be done in earth, as it is in heaven."
— Matthew 6:10 (KJV)

"The LORD shall send the rod of Thy strength out of Zion: rule
Thou in the midst of Thine enemies."
— Psalm 110:2 (KJV)

"For the LORD is our Judge, the LORD is our Lawgiver,
the LORD is our King; He will save us."
— Isaiah 33:22 (KJV)

SABBATH FIRE

CONTENTS

FOREWORD

Every generation is marked by a moment when heaven interrupts the noise of history and restores the original blueprint.
We are living in such a moment now.

For centuries, the Church has been defined by what she *does:* her programs, her buildings, her gatherings, her traditions.
But heaven has always defined her by who she *is:*
the governmental Body of Christ, the executive expression of the King, the living tribunal of Zion.

This book does not merely repeat this truth; it **awakens** it.

Here, the Church is not presented as an institution limping through culture, but as a fire-forged government standing above culture.
Here, the believer is not a passive attendee but a legislative son carrying keys, seals, verdicts, and dominion.
Here, the Sabbath is not a only day; it is the throne where God rests in His people.
Here, judgment is not destruction; it is alignment.
Here, worship is not music; it is governance.

What you hold in your hands is not commentary.
It is not entertainment.
It is not another voice in an overcrowded marketplace of opinions.
It is a **mandate**.

The author brings a clarity rarely seen in this age; a clarity born

not from academic detachment but from prophetic encounter.
He reads Scripture as a governmental constitution.
He handles revelation like a legislator, not a theorist.
He writes with the urgency of one who has seen the throne and cannot remain silent.

Page after page, you will feel heaven's architecture rise around you, line upon line, precept upon precept; until you stand inside the mystery Isaiah foresaw and John witnessed: **the Lamb enthroned, the saints ascending, the nations trembling awake.**

This work calls the Church out of survival-mode Christianity and into throne-room identity.
It shifts the believer from spectator to steward, from member to magistrate, from worshipper to governor.

If you let these pages speak deeply, they will not only inform your mind; they will recalibrate your life.

Read slowly.
Read prayerfully.
Read ready to be changed.

Because once the Ekklesia understands who she really is, the gates of hell do not stand a chance.

Welcome to the unveiling of the **True Church — the Undisputed Government of Heaven on Earth.**

INTRODUCTION

The Word Ekklesia: Heaven's
Original Blueprint for Dominion

Before a cross was lifted, before a pulpit was carved, Christ spoke a constitutional word that reshaped the destiny of creation:

> *"Upon this rock I will build My ekklesia, and the gates of hell shall not prevail against it." — Matthew 16:18*

This was not religious poetry. It was legislation.

The term *ekklesia* in the mouth of Jesus was not borrowed from synagogue language. It was a political word, the very term used for Greece's ruling assembly, where citizens gathered to deliberate and decree on behalf of the state. To the ears of the disciples, it did not mean *a building of worshipers*, but *a governing council of citizens called out to legislate the will of their kingdom*.

When Christ declared "I will build My ekklesia," He was not founding a religion; He was reestablishing divine government on earth. Adam had forfeited it; Christ reclaimed it. The Kingdom of God is not a subject of study; it is a jurisdiction. And the Church is its parliament.

1. The Misunderstanding of "Church"

The English word *church*, derived from *kyriakon*, "belonging to the Lord," subtly shifted the meaning. Over time, *ekklesia* was

reduced from a governing assembly to a religious meeting. The throne became a stage; the gavel became a microphone.
Buildings replaced councils. Sermons replaced decrees. Membership replaced citizenship.

Thus, what was meant to rule began to perform. The Church, stripped of its governmental nature, settled for attendance rather than dominion. The gates of hell did not tremble before a crowd; they fear only a court seated in the name of the King.

2. From Congregation to Council

The ekklesia is not merely "called out," it is "called up." It operates from the mountain, not the valley. It does not wait for permission from men, for it was born in the eternal counsel of God. Its authority is derived not from numbers but from alignment.
In heaven's design, a congregation gathers around inspiration; a council gathers around instruction.
One listens, the other legislates.
The true Church hears from heaven and translates that word into earthly law through prayer, decree, and obedience.

In the courtroom of Zion, every believer is summoned as both priest and king; to worship and to govern. Prayer is not begging; it is participation in divine legislation. When the Spirit says, *"Whatsoever you bind on earth shall be bound in heaven,"* He is describing a courtroom protocol; the binding of verdicts, the sealing of decrees, the release of judgments from the throne.

3. The Voice of Christ in Matthew 16:18 — A Constitutional Decree

Christ's statement at Caesarea Philippi was a royal proclamation. He stood before the very region known for idol worship and territorial spirits, announcing the rise of a new order. When He said, *"I will build My ekklesia,"* it was heaven declaring independence from the systems of men. It was not the promise of an organisation but the constitution of a Kingdom.

The *rock* was not Peter's personality but the revelation of Christ's identity. Upon that revelation, "Thou art the Christ, the Son of the Living God", rests the foundation of every governmental decree in heaven's court.

He did not say, *"I will build My temple,"* but *"My ekklesia."*
He was not speaking of architecture, but authority.
Not of religion, but reign.

The true Church is heaven's embassy on earth; an assembly that carries the constitution of the Kingdom, enforces divine verdicts, and manifests heaven's government in human form.

When this revelation returns to the body, the walls of religion will fall, and the courtroom of heaven will reopen in the midst of the saints.

PREFACE

*The Call to Rise: When Religion
Crumbles and Government Emerges*

There comes a time when heaven no longer negotiates with tradition. A time when the Spirit walks into the ruins of religion and calls forth a remnant; not to build another denomination, but to awaken a government. The shaking of the visible church is not destruction; it is divine demolition. Every structure built by ambition, culture, and compromise must fall so that what is of the Kingdom may stand.

The voice of the Spirit is crying again, "Come up hither." The ekklesia is not a crowd gathered around a pulpit, but a council seated around a throne. The true Church was never meant to be a sanctuary for spectators, but a courtroom of witnesses. It does not wait for permission from men, for it is born from decree. It does not operate from earth to heaven, but from heaven to earth.

Religion gathers; government governs. One builds walls; the other opens gates. The true Church is not seen by the carnal eye because it is spiritual, governmental, and judicial — established upon revelation and ruled by the Spirit of Truth.

This call is personal. It comes like fire upon those tired of powerless sermons and empty rituals. It comes to those who have seen the veil tear and refuse to sew it back. It is the awakening of kings and priests who understand that to worship is to legislate, and to intercede is to issue decrees from Zion's courtroom.

What is arising now is not revival: it is resurrection.
The Lord is not returning for a religious institution, but for a governmental bride clothed with judgment and burning, purified to reign with Him.

This book is not an argument. It is a summons.
A call to those who hear the sound of heaven's gavel striking the altar — "The case of the nations is open."
And the Spirit is gathering His witnesses, His royal court, His true ekklesia.

PROLOGUE

When Heaven Stands Up

Before the foundations of the world were framed, governance was not an idea; it was a Presence.
The throne was not crafted; it *was*.
Light was the first legislation.
Breath was the first decree.
Glory was the first constitution.

When God spoke, creation aligned.
When He rested, creation stabilised.
When He moved, creation advanced.

But when He formed man, He revealed His long-hidden strategy:
Heaven would rule on earth through a Body, not a bureaucracy.

This Body would bear His name, host His Spirit, transmit His will, and execute His judgments with precision.
This Body would stand in the gaps where nations collapse, speak where kings fall silent, and burn where darkness gathers.
This Body would be mobile Zion, the living mountain of the Lord.
This Body would be unstoppable.

And so the ancient war intensified.
Not because the adversary feared religion, but because he feared government.
Not because he trembled at worship, but because he trembled at *authority*.

Not because he opposed gatherings, but because he opposed *Ekklesia*.

Through ages of distortion, persecution, empire, compromise, and silence, a remnant kept the blueprint.
A people who refused to bow to systems, shadows, or substitutes.
A people who carried fire in their bones and verdicts in their mouths.
A people who remembered that the Church is not a building, not a brand, not an event; but **the governmental Body of the enthroned Christ.**

Now, in the final movements of history, Heaven is standing up again.
Thrones are shifting.
Altars are answering.
Scrolls are opening.
The Spirit is summoning His true House to its original mandate.

This book is not information; it is activation.
It is not theory; it is legislation.
It is not commentary; it is a call to ascend.

You are stepping into the architecture of God's government; a government that cannot be voted out, silenced, diluted, or defeated.
A government built on righteousness, fuelled by glory, and sustained by eternal rest.

Welcome to the revelation of the **True Church — the Undisputed Government of Heaven on Earth.**

The scroll is open.
The throne is speaking.
Let the Ekklesia arise.

PART I

*THE REVELATION OF
THE ECCLESIA*

CHAPTER 1

Born of Breath, Not Brick

Spiritology of the Ekklesia — The Breath That Builds

*B*efore there was ever a church building, there was a breathing. *Before men ever gathered in temples, the Spirit hovered over waters. The true ekklesia is not founded in mortar or stone; it is born of breath.*

When Jesus said, "Upon this rock I will build My church," (**Matthew 16:18**), He was not speaking of architecture but of *atmosphere;* a spiritual constitution formed by revelation, not religion. The first Church was not in Jerusalem, Antioch, or Rome. It was in Eden, when God *breathed* into Adam, and man became a living soul (**Genesis 2:7**). That breath — *ruach* — was the Spirit's governmental signature, the seal of divine authority that made man heaven's representative on earth.

Thus, the *ekklesia* was never meant to be a building that gathers bodies, but a body that carries heaven. The walls of the Spirit replaced the walls of stone. Every time man tries to contain the Spirit within structures, the wind breaks out and breathes again. Pentecost was not the beginning of a denomination; it was the restoration of Eden's breath — the same Spirit that hovered, now dwelling in man again.

Religion builds temples; the Spirit builds testimonies. Religion fills pews; the Spirit fills people. The *ekklesia* cannot be franchised or replicated; it is born of those who are breathed upon.

The First Calling Out — From Genesis to Pentecost

The word *ekklesia* means "the called-out ones." But called out from what? From confusion to order. From earth's noise to heaven's decree. From man's assembly to God's council.

The first *calling out* was not in the book of Acts; it began when God called Adam out from the dust. The Spirit separated him from earth's chaos and crowned him with dominion. When Noah was called out of the flood, Abraham out of Ur, Moses out of Egypt, and Israel out of bondage, the pattern remained the same: *God calls out to call forth.*

Each calling is a step toward Pentecost, where the full circle closes. In Genesis, man was formed from dust and filled with Spirit; in Acts, the Church was formed from prayer and filled with fire. The Spirit that once dwelt *with* man now dwelt *in* man, and the divine government was reborn.

From breath to wind, from Eden to upper room; this is the progressive revelation of the *ekklesia*. It is not an organisation evolving through history, but a Spirit lineage continuing through eternity.

How Religion Replaced Revelation

The greatest threat to the *ekklesia* has never been persecution; it is *institutionalisation*. When men lose the revelation of the Spirit, they begin to build monuments around memories. They confuse *attendance* with *ascension* and *membership* with *citizens hip.*

After Constantine legalised Christianity, the *ekklesia* was reduced to an earthly hierarchy; bishops, cathedrals, and ceremonies replaced breath, revelation, and power. The Church that was meant to *govern* began to *perform*. The presence that once flowed freely was now caged behind golden altars.

But revelation cannot be buried. Every time religion tries to bury truth, resurrection comes. Every reformer, prophet, and revival was a reminder: *the Spirit still breathes.* The true Church cannot be governed by earthly kings; it is ruled from the throne in heaven.

Revelation is the currency of heaven's government. The *ekklesia* loses authority the moment it trades revelation for ritual. The Spirit of Truth is the constitution, not creeds written by men.

The Holy Spirit — Governor of the Kingdom

In every kingdom, there is a governor; one who represents the will of the king in every province. In God's Kingdom, that Governor is the Holy Spirit. He is the living Constitution who administrates heaven's will on earth.

When Christ ascended, He did not leave us religion; He sent government, *the Spirit of Truth* (**John 16:13**). The same Spirit that empowered creation now empowers re-creation. The Governor's purpose is to train citizens to rule as sons, to legislate from the court of Zion, and to manifest heaven's law through love.

Without the Spirit, the Church becomes a democracy of opinions. With the Spirit, it becomes a monarchy of revelation. The Holy Spirit does not negotiate votes; He enforces decrees. He is heaven's witness within us, bearing record of the Son (*1 John 5:7–8*).

Thus, the *ekklesia* is not an earthly organisation under human administration; it is a divine embassy governed by the Spirit of God. Every believer is a living chamber of His rule, a breathing temple of His government.

7-Dimensional Breakdown of the True Ekklesia

Dimension	Expression	Description
Spiritology	The Breath	The Church as the living embodiment of divine Spirit, animated by heaven's breath.
Soulogy	The Council	The inner mind of Christ ruling through unity, harmony, and wisdom of His people.
Physiology	The Body	The physical manifestation of God's order — believers as vessels and extensions of His will.
Theology	The Covenant	The divine framework of rulership established through Christ's blood and Word.
Chronology	The Continuum	The progression from Eden's breath to Pentecostal fire, tracing heaven's unfolding government.

| Typology | The Pattern | Every exodus, altar, and temple foreshadowing the final spiritual *ekklesia*. |
| Technology | The Administration | The operation of divine systems — prayer, prophecy, decree — by the Spirit's interface in man. |

Prophetic Charge:

"You are not called to attend; you are called to ascend.
You are not built of brick but born of breath.
You are the living house of His decree; the ekklesia, the
breath that governs."

CHAPTER 2

The Throne Within

The Soul as the Seat of Government

*E*very throne has a seat. Every government has a centre. *The ekklesia begins not in a cathedral but within the chambers of the soul. The soul is the seat of government; the meeting point where heaven's decrees descend and earth's realities respond.*

When God breathed into Adam, He did not build a temple of marble; He enthroned Himself within a consciousness. The soul became the inner court of divine administration, where intellect, emotion, and will must bow before Spirit.

Lucifer fell because he exalted his *will* above the divine. Adam fell because he listened to another *voice* above revelation. Redemption, therefore, restores government within, not first without.

The true *ekklesia* cannot govern nations until it governs thought. Every rebellion on earth begins in an unrenewed mind. Every restoration in the Spirit begins in a soul surrendered to divine law. The mind is not merely a battlefield; it is a *throne room*.

Whoever sits upon it rules the man.

Christ reigns not through external force but internal submission; *"Let this mind be in you, which was also in Christ Jesus"* (**Philippians 2:5**). When the mind is renewed, the throne is restored.

Renewal of the Mind as Enthronement

Renewal is not education; it is enthronement. When Paul declared, *"Be transformed by the renewing of your mind"* (**Romans 12:2**), he was declaring a coronation, not a classroom. The mind renewed by revelation becomes the lawful seat of Christ's dominion.

The fallen mind is an usurped throne, ruled by fear, lust, and pride: all illegal governments in the soul's territory. The Holy Spirit enters as the *Governor* to evict the false kings and restore lawful order.

Each revelation you receive is a decree of enthronement. Each truth obeyed becomes a sceptre extended. Transformation is not a feeling; it is jurisdictional expansion; the territory of heaven being reclaimed within.

To renew the mind is to reinstall heaven's constitution in the inner court. To meditate upon the Word is to let the gavel of God strike within your thoughts. The Word does not merely inform; it legislates.

Thus, when the *ekklesia* prays, decrees, and intercedes, its authority flows from this inner enthronement. Without inner government, there is no outer dominion.

Dominion Through Alignment

True dominion is not conquest; it is *alignment*. Dominion is the effortless authority that flows when heaven and earth agree;

when Spirit, soul, and body stand in divine order.

Adam lost dominion the moment his soul disagreed with Spirit. Jesus restored dominion because His will never disagreed with the Father. He said, *"I do nothing of Myself, but as My Father hath taught Me, I speak these things"* (**John 8:28**).

Dominion is therefore not achieved through striving but through synchronisation; when the throne within echoes the throne above. When your soul says "Yes" to heaven's decree, power flows like lightning.

The aligned man becomes an embassy of divine authority. Angels recognise that alignment as legal order. Demons flee not because of noise but because of jurisdiction. When heaven and soul are one, words become law.

That is why Jesus could speak to storms, trees, and death itself: He was in perfect alignment with the government of the Father. Dominion is not domination; it is a demonstration of divine order through obedience.

When the *ekklesia* aligns, creation responds. The Spirit within man governs the matter around man. The voice of a renewed soul carries the resonance of Zion's throne.

The Mystery of Inner Zion

Zion is not a mountain in the Middle East; it is the mountain within. It is the spiritual high place of communion where the Spirit and soul unite in covenant rest.

David looked toward physical Zion, but Christ awakens *inner Zion;* the throne of the Spirit within the heart. *"The Lord hath chosen Zion; He hath desired it for His habitation"* (**Psalm 132:13**). Zion is not visited; it is indwelt.

When the Holy Spirit took residence within man, the prophecy of Zion shifted from geography to anatomy. The heart became the holy hill; the mind, the temple courts; the spirit, the most holy place. The *ekklesia* is thus the manifestation of Zion; the inner government of God expressed through a collective body.

In inner Zion, worship is legislation, prayer is deliberation, and prophecy is decree. Here, the Lamb sits as Judge, the Spirit as Witness, and the Word as Law. This is the courtroom within every believer, where cases of thought and motive are tried by the light of truth.

The mystery of inner Zion is that heaven is no longer distant. The throne of God is now in you, and you are seated with Christ *in heavenly places* (**Ephesians 2:6**). Dominion is therefore not ascension upward but awareness inward.

To ascend the hill of the Lord is to yield to the Spirit's government within. When inner Zion rules, outer Babylon collapses.

7-Dimensional Breakdown — The Throne Within

Dimension	Expression	Description
Spiritology	The Breath of Rule	The Spirit is the indwelling King establishing His dominion in the inner man.
Soulogy	The Seat of Counsel	The mind and emotions transformed into instruments of divine decree.
Physiology	The Vessel of Manifestation	The body is the visible domain where the inner government demonstrates itself.

Theology	The Covenant of Kingship	The Word as constitution restoring lawful order in man's inner kingdom.
Chronology	From Eden to Zion	The progression from the lost throne in Adam to the restored throne in Christ.
Typology	The Tabernacle Within	Spirit as Most Holy, Soul as Holy Place, Body as Outer Court.
Technology	The Operation of Renewal	The mechanisms of transformation: meditation, decree, alignment, and obedience as tools of spiritual governance.

Prophetic Courtroom Imagery

The soul stands before the throne within. The Spirit enters as Judge, the Word as Witness, the conscience as Jury. Every thought is tried, every emotion weighed. The verdict is alignment or rebellion. When alignment is chosen, the gavel falls — Dominion granted.

Prophetic Charge

> *"Throne of God, arise within me.*
> *Let every false king fall.*
> *Let my thoughts bow before Truth,*
> *My will merge with Yours,*

Until my soul becomes Your seat,
And Zion burns from within."

CHAPTER 3

The Body as a Living Temple

Physiology of Divine Structure

*T*he ekklesia was never designed as a monument of stone but as an organism of spirit and life. Every believer is not a brick but a living cell within the body of Christ; a breathing stone, pulsating with divine intelligence. The structure of the Church follows the same pattern as the human body: it is animated by one breath, coordinated by one head, and sustained by one bloodstream — the Spirit.

Paul revealed this mystery with anatomical precision:

> **"For as the body is one, and hath many members... so also is Christ." — 1 Corinthians 12:12**

He did not say "so also is the Church," but *so also is Christ.* Meaning — the *ekklesia* is the continuation of His incarnation. The same Word that took on flesh in one Man now takes on form in many. The divine physiology is collective; Spirit woven through soul and matter, the invisible made visible through unity.

Every part holds intelligence, purpose, and priestly function. The eye discerns, the ear hears, the hand serves, the heart burns. The body is not merely symbolic; it is a functional government. The Spirit flows through it like an electrical current through a living circuit.

Where religion builds walls, divine physiology builds connections. The Church is not a franchise of local assemblies but a network of nerves and veins through which the mind of Christ coordinates heaven's activity on earth.

Priestly Networks in the Body of Christ

Every member is both a vessel and a voice. The priesthood of believers is not a slogan; it is a network — a system of spiritual conductivity that allows divine current to move from one to another.

The *ekklesia* operates as a living organism of priestly order. Some are altars of intercession; others are trumpets of prophecy; others, vessels of mercy or swords of truth. Yet all are synchronised through one High Priest who ministers in the heavens — Christ Jesus.

When one prays, another is empowered. When one suffers, the entire system feels the tremor. Such is the sensitivity of divine design. The blood of Christ, spiritually speaking, is the Spirit moving through every joint and ligament, cleansing, healing, and quickening.

Each believer is an altar point, and when these altars connect, the global *ekklesia* forms one priestly circuit. Intercession rises like incense, decree flows like breath, and government manifests like light.

To neglect fellowship is to sever nerve and vein; it is a form of spiritual amputation. The enemy isolates to disable function; the Spirit unites to restore power.

The priestly network of the body is heaven's operating system on earth. The Spirit is the signal; holiness is the conductivity; love is the voltage.

The Altar as the Heart of Government

If the body is the temple, the heart is the altar.

The altar is not furniture; it is a function — the place where exchange happens between realms. Every true act of worship is a transaction of government: surrender releases authority, sacrifice invites reign, fire answers order.

From Genesis onward, every altar marked a legal portal of dominion. Abel's altar established divine acceptance; Noah's altar restructured the earth; Abraham's altar birthed a covenant; Christ's cross — the final altar — opened eternity itself.

In the *ekklesia*, the heart of every believer becomes the altar where the Spirit legislates mercy and truth. The flame that once fell on Sinai now burns inwardly, turning prayer into incense and obedience into offering.

When the corporate heart of the body beats in rhythm with the Lamb, heaven's verdicts pulse through the earth. Revelation calls this the *golden altar before the throne*, where the prayers of the saints rise as incense (**Revelation 8:3–4**). The true altar is thus not built, but born, out of hearts yielded to the government of the Spirit.

Where hearts are divided, government collapses. Where hearts are one, the altar becomes a throne.

The Operation of the Spirit Through Members

The operation of the Spirit within the *ekklesia* is not random inspiration but coordinated administration. Paul described this in *1 Corinthians 12*: "There are diversities of operations, but it is the same God which worketh all in all."

The Spirit operates like breath through a living organism; inhaling revelation, exhaling manifestation. Each member, when aligned, becomes an extension of divine motion.

Through the prophetic, He speaks.
Through the apostolic, He builds.
Through the pastoral, He heals.
Through the evangelistic, He reaches.
Through the teaching, He anchors.

These are not titles; they are functions of breath. When the Spirit exhales through one, others inhale and continue the flow. The government of God operates through circulation, not hierarchy.

Where the Spirit is grieved, the flow halts. Where unity reigns, the current intensifies. Thus, the vitality of the *ekklesia* depends not on programs but on breath; the Holy Spirit continually animating, coordinating, and renewing.

The Spirit is not an accessory to the Church; He *is* the Church in motion. Without Him, structure decays. With Him, even dry bones form armies.

7-Dimensional Breakdown — The Body as a Living Temple

Dimension	Expression	Description
Spiritology	Breath as Life	The Holy Spirit animates and unites all members into one living organism.

Soulogy	Coordination of Will	Collective submission and love synchronise the body's movements.
Physiology	Temple Anatomy	The Church mirrors the body; heart as altar, mind as holy place, hands and feet as instruments.
Theology	Incarnation Extended	Christ continues His incarnation through His corporate body on earth.
Chronology	From Adam to Christ to Ekklesia	The shift from individual vessels to a collective temple of the Spirit.
Typology	The Tabernacle Fulfilled	The outer court, holy place, and most holy place fulfilled in body, soul, and spirit.
Technology	Operation of Breath	Spiritual functions (gifts, ministries, decrees) as the systems that regulate divine life-flow.

Prophetic Courtroom Imagery

Heaven convenes its council not in marble halls but in bodies surrendered. Each member is a witness, each gift is a law, each act of obedience is a verdict enforced. When the altar of hearts burns in agreement, the Spirit moves through the body like fire through gold, purging, empowering, and legislating from within.

Prophetic Charge

"Spirit of the Living God, breathe through Your body.
Unite the scattered nerves of Your people.
Let every heart become an altar,
Every word a decree,
Every member a vessel of Your flame.
Let the living temple rise —
Not built by hands,
But born by Breath."

CHAPTER 4

Christic the Constitution and King

Theological Basis of Heavenly Rule

*B*efore there were angels, stars, or worlds, there was government. Order is older than creation. Dominion did not begin in Eden; it was eternal in the nature of God.

The Kingdom of Heaven is not a democracy of opinions but a monarchy of righteousness. Its rule is built upon the divine harmony of three: the Father who wills, the Son who embodies, and the Spirit who executes. This is not hierarchy; it is perfect unity in operation, government flowing as life, not as control.

At the heart of this government is **Christ**, the living Constitution. The Word of God is not simply a document of law but a Person in whom every statute, covenant, and promise finds its breath.

"In the beginning was the Word, and the Word was with God, and the Word was God." —John 1:1

Every kingdom is defined by its constitution, the legal embodiment of its will. For heaven, that constitution is Christ Himself. To know Him is to know the law of life; to disobey Him is to reject divine order.

The Church cannot operate in true authority apart from conformity to this Constitution. Revelation without Christ is rebellion disguised as zeal. Every doctrine, gift, and manifestation must trace back to the living Word, the law written not on parchment but in blood.

The Father enthroned Him, the Spirit confirms Him, and all creation bows before Him. Christ is the decree and the enforcement, the foundation and the crown.

"He upholds all things by the Word of His power." — *Hebrews 1:3*

It does not say *the power of His Word* but *the Word of His power* — meaning the Person of Christ sustains all dominion. The power is alive, not abstract.

The Father as Judge, the Son as King, the Spirit as Executor

Every lawful government operates through three branches: legislation, execution, and judgment. Heaven mirrors this order perfectly:

- **The Father as Judge** — the source of will and justice.

- **The Son as King** — the manifestation of that will in dominion.

- **The Spirit as Executor** — the power that enforces the verdicts of heaven on earth.

This is the divine order revealed throughout Scripture. The

Father decrees, the Son embodies, the Spirit performs.

At Christ's baptism, this triune court convened visibly: the Father's voice spoke from heaven, the Son stood in the Jordan, and the Spirit descended like a dove. Government re-entered the earth through perfect alignment.

When Jesus declared, *"All authority in heaven and on earth has been given to Me,"* He was not boasting: He was restoring the chain of command. The Son does nothing of Himself; the Spirit takes nothing of His own; the Father judges through both.

Thus, in every act of true spiritual governance, this order must remain intact. The Church legislates only as it listens to the Father, decrees only as it abides in the Son, and enforces only as it yields to the Spirit.

Disorder in this triune flow births religion, control, and confusion. The enemy mimics this structure: false fatherhood (tyranny), false kingship (pride), false spirit (deception). Only alignment with divine government brings righteousness and peace.

The Threefold Order: Prophet, Teacher, Apostle

Heaven's government extends its operation through earthly offices, divine expressions of its triune order:

- **The Prophet** carries the voice of the *Judge*. He hears divine verdicts and proclaims them.

- **The Teacher** embodies the *Law*, preserving accuracy and continuity in truth.

- **The Apostle** enforces the *King's dominion*, establishing order and culture in territories.

Prophets reveal God's intention. Teachers codify it. Apostles implement it.

Together, they mirror the rhythm of Father, Son, and Spirit. Prophecy without teaching becomes zeal without structure. Teaching without apostolic authority becomes intellect without enforcement. Apostolic work without prophetic or teaching roots becomes an empire, not a Kingdom.

The true *ekklesia* is built upon this threefold cord.

> *"And God hath set some in the church, first apostles, secondarily prophets, thirdly teachers..."* — *1 Corinthians 12:28*

When these functions operate in harmony, heaven's law becomes visible on earth. The Spirit flows through their unity as power flows through a circuit. Revelation becomes law; law becomes culture; culture becomes dominion.

This is the architecture of divine civilisation, not built by human strategy but by divine sequence.

Isaiah 33:22 — The Foundation of Spiritual Government

> *"For the LORD is our Judge, the LORD is our Lawgiver, the LORD is our King; He will save us."* — *Isaiah 33:22*

This single verse is the spine of divine government. It reveals heaven's judicial, legislative, and executive branches united in one Lord.

- **Judge** — the Father, source of justice.

- **Lawgiver** — the Son, Word made flesh.

- **King** — the Spirit, executing the rule through the body.

Isaiah saw what men now teach as theology: the *ekklesia* as the governmental vessel of a threefold God. When these dimensions converge in a man, a people, or a nation, salvation manifests: *"He will save us."*

The Church is not merely saved from sin but saved into government, restored to the order of divine rulership. Every prayer becomes a case presented before the Judge, every teaching a statute inscribed, every decree a royal enactment from the throne.

Heaven's courtroom is not a metaphor; it is the atmosphere of divine order. And *Isaiah 33:22* is its constitution in miniature.

The apostolic age is not the age of preachers but of governments; men and women seated in Christ, ruling by righteousness and mercy. Salvation without governance is incomplete redemption.

7-Dimensional Breakdown — Christ the Constitution and King

Dimension	Expression	Description
Spiritology	Breath of Dominion	The Spirit enforces Christ's kingship through believers, establishing divine order.
Soulogy	Law Written Within	The mind and heart internalize Christ as the constitution of life.
Physiology	Incarnate Structure	The body becomes the vessel of royal enactment — the Word lived, not spoken only.
Theology	Christ as	He is the Word, the Lawgiver,

	Constitution	and the embodiment of divine justice.
Chronology	From Creation to Coronation	The government of God revealed from Eden's mandate to the Lamb's throne.
Typology	Prophet, Teacher, and Apostle	Earthly reflections of the triune order in divine administration.
Technology	Judicial Operation	Prayer, decree, prophecy, and teaching as instruments of heavenly governance.

Prophetic Courtroom Imagery

The throne room is convened. The Father presides as Judge, the Son stands as the Word of the Law, the Spirit moves as living Fire executing the decree. Before them, the saints stand — not as defendants, but as co-governors. The gavel falls, the seals break, and the Kingdom advances one verdict at a time.

Prophetic Charge

"O Christ, my Constitution and my King,
Write Your law in my reins and heart.
Let Your statutes govern my thoughts,
Your judgments direct my words,
And Your Spirit enforce Your reign within me.

Make me an article of Your covenant,
A vessel of Your order,
A citizen of Your court.
For You alone are Judge, Lawgiver, and King
And You will save us."

PART II

THE GOVERNMENT OF ZION

CHAPTER 5

Zion in Session: The Courtroom of Heaven

Opening Statement — The Hall Is Called

When the ekklesia assembles in Spirit and truth, she is not meeting for a program; she is convening a court. Psalm 82 declares, "God standeth in the congregation of the mighty; he judgeth among the gods." The picture is legal: a throne, a bench, witnesses, accusers, pleadings, and a record. Daniel sees scrolls opened and books inspected as multitudes stand before the Ancient of Days. This chapter walks through that courtroom; its architecture, its pleadings, its recorders, and its enforcers, because the remnant must learn to prosecute the case of the nations.

I. The Architecture of Divine Judgment

Heaven's courtroom is not a cold hall of law; it is a living, relational architecture made of person and presence.

1. **The Bench (The Throne):** The Father presides as Judge, but the bench extends; the Son is the embodied law, the Spirit the active judicial officer. The bench issues verdicts that ripple through time.

2. **The Counsel (Intercessors & Prophets):** Those who stand before the bench do not beg; they plead a case. They present evidence (the Word, testimony, covenant), examine witnesses (angels, scriptures, testimonies), and petition for enforcement.

3. **The Bar (Priestly Network):** A functional network of altars, intercessory cells, prophetic offices, and apostolic courts; this is the legal counsel of Zion.

4. **The Docket (Cases of the Nations):** Each city, family, and territory is a case on heaven's docket. Prayer is the filling. Decrees are the rulings. Enforcement follows the sealed verdict.

5. **The Record Room (Books and Scrolls):** Every petition, oath, and act is recorded. The books that Daniel saw are not metaphors alone; they are legal archives used for enforcement.

The architecture is designed for the verdicts to move from heaven into manifest reality. The pattern is orderly: Revelation → Pleading → Verdict → Enforcement.

II. Intercession as Legal Pleading

Intercession is not emotional overflow; it is a legal calling.

- **Filing the Case:** Intercession begins by naming the case: a person, a family, a city. The intercessor summons heaven to hear evidence rooted in covenant and promise.

- **Presentation of Evidence:** Scripture is admitted as legal testimony. Righteous acts, covenant claims, blood, remembrance, and repentant hearts are all material evidence.

- **Cross-Examination:** The accuser (Satan) will bring charges: fear, accusation, and generational sin. Intercession answers by exposing the accuser's case, applying the blood, and calling witnesses (memory of God's past acts).

- **Pleading the Covenant:** Great lawyers of Zion plead covenantal language: promises to Abraham, Christ's victory, and covenant statutes. They do not barter; they remind heaven of its own word.

- **Motion for Enforcement:** A petition ends with a motion: "Let the verdict be executed." This is the decree. It is not repeated as vain wish, but issued as legal mandate.

A courtroom intercession uses structure: silence to hear the Judge; petition to present the issue; witness to affirm the claim; decree to seal the action. When the ekklesia learns pleadings, prayer moves from wish to warrant.

III. Angels as Recorders and Enforcers of Verdicts

Heaven's legal staff are not abstract forces; they are persons with portfolios.

- **Recorders:** Angels keep minutes. They carry the books. Every oath and every declaration is logged. This is why confession, testimony, and accurate proclamation matter; wrong entries can confuse enforcement.

- **Messengers:** Angels transport decrees from heaven to territory. They open doors, close mouths, and arrange encounters. They are the King's couriers responding to sealed warrants.

- **Enforcers:** Some angels execute judgments. They do not act on whim; they act on law. When heaven's gavel falls, they move with exactness to correct the created order.

- **Advocates and Counsellors:** Angels also stand to witness and to testify to the integrity of the case. They can present prior acts of God as precedent to secure verdicts.

Practically: treat angelic ministry as judicial staff. Feed them with accurate declarations, send them with clear decrees, and expect legal enforcement. Their activity respects procedure.

IV. Psalm 82 and Daniel 7 in Operation — Seeing the Text Move

Psalm 82 positions God standing "in the congregation of the mighty", judging among lesser powers. *Daniel 7* shows books opened before the Ancient of Days, and thrones set. These are not poetic metaphors only; they are procedural descriptions.

- *Psalm 82* **in operation:** God judges corruption among the "gods" (powers and principalities). The ekklesia's role is to bring the case against unjust spiritual governance. Local altars must call heaven's attention to every form of idolatry that holds a region captive.

- *Daniel 7* **in operation:** Courts convene; books are opened; sentences are given against oppressive powers. This is the procedural moment when prophetic evidence collates into an enforceable sentence.

When these texts move, you will observe: sudden release (open prisons), judicial reversals (shifts in leadership), and legal nullification of covenants that oppress nations (breakings of ungodly power). Expect formality; the Spirit respects process.

V. Courtroom Forms — A Practical Flow for Zion in Session

Use this as a template in corporate sessions:

1. **Call to Order:** Silence; reverence; invitation for Father's presiding presence. (Seat the Judge.)

2. **Presentation of Case:** Name the matter; read covenantal claims and scriptural precedent. (File the case.)

3. **Witness Testimony:** Cite testimonies, prophetic words, and

historical acts from God. (Call witnesses.)

4. **Cross-Examination of the Accuser:** Expose lies, generational patterns, and legal infractions. (Discredit the charge.)

5. **Plea for Judgment:** Declare the specific relief sought (deliverance, dismantling, reversal). (Motion.)

6. **Sealing the Verdict:** Corporate decree — spoken, written, and signed by anointed leaders. (Seal.)

7. **Dispatch of Enforcement:** Invoke angelic ministry for execution and give clear legal instructions. (Serve warrant.)

8. **Report to the Record Room:** Proclaim the outcome and register testimony for future verification. (Record.)

9. **Adjournment with Praise:** Worship as the release of enforcement energy; thanksgiving as the final seal.

This is a courtroom liturgy, not a theatrical ritual. Keep it sober, covenantal, and focused on procedure.

VI. The Standards of Evidence — What Holds Up in Zion's Court

Heaven's court admits certain kinds of evidence:

- **The Word:** Written revelation is admissible and carries highest weight. Scriptural promises are precedents.

- **Covenant Acts:** Past interventions by God on behalf of a people are admissible as precedent.

- **Repentance and Obedience:** Where people repent and align, heaven typically responds favourably.

- **The Blood:** The legal efficacy of Christ's blood annuls illegitimate claims.

- **Prophetic Witness:** Spirit-breathed revelation that aligns with Scripture is sworn testimony.

- **Corporate Decree:** Unified, covenantal decrees carry executive weight.

Anything lacking these standards may be delayed. The Spirit enforces what is lawful; passion alone does not satisfy procedure.

VII. 7-Dimensional Breakdown — Zion in Session

Dimension	Expression	Application in Court
Spiritology	Judicial Breath	The Spirit convenes and authenticates the session.
Soulogy	Inner Counsel	The mind and heart present coherent, covenantal pleas.
Physiology	Priestly Network	Bodies aligned with roles operate the courtroom functions.
Theology	Covenant Law	The Word provides statutes, precedents, and legal claims.
Chronology	Legal Timeline	Cases may span generations; history is part of evidence.
Typology	Patterns of Justice	Old Testament cases (Abraham, Moses, Daniel) illustrate procedure.

Technology	Enforcement Systems	Angelic logistics, prophetic decrees, and recorded verdicts as mechanisms of execution.

VIII. Case Studies — How Courtroom Sessions Play Out (Prophetic Examples)

1. **Family Lineage Case:** A household sits, names generational curses, presents repentance and covenant claims, calls witnesses (grandparents' testimonies of God's mercy), and decrees reversal. Result: pattern broken, marriages restored, ancestral altar dismantled.

2. **City Docket:** An assembly files the case against corruption in civic leadership: evidence (exposure of injustice), prophetic precedent (word for the city), and prayerful pleading. Result: sudden resignations, new leaders arise, civic structures reform.

3. **Spiritual Stronghold:** The ekklesia sues the stronghold of addiction: they call witnesses (former captives), present the blood's power, decree freedom, and dispatch angelic enforcement. Result: mass deliverance and new ministries birthed.

These are not magic formulas but legal precedents. They require covenant, procedure, and the Spirit's sanction.

IX. The Risk and the Reward — Why Courts Scare the Untrained

Two things happen in heaven's court: exposure and healing. The untrained fear because exposure often comes before correction. But correction is the path to restoration. The reward is that God's government replaces thralldom with rule. The ekklesia that sits in court learns to read records, move on warrants, and shepherd nations.

X. Prophetic Charge — The Gavel Falls

"Arise, O lawful assembly.
Take Your seats in heaven's bench.
File the case for the widow, the orphan, the land.
Present the covenant. Call the witnesses.
Let the books be opened; let the gavel fall.
Send forth Your messengers; execute what You have sealed.
Justice, Justice — You shall pursue until the earth is full of the knowledge of the Lord."

XI. Decree & Template — A Practical Courtroom Decree (Editable)

We, the assembled ekklesia of [*place/name*], standing in covenant with the Father, by the authority of Jesus Christ and the testimony of the Holy Spirit, do hereby present the case of [*description*]. Based upon the Word ([*scripture reference*]), the blood of the Lamb, and the precedent of God's covenant, we plead for the following verdict: [*specific legal outcomes — e.g., release, reversal, restoration, resignation*]. We seal this verdict with our unified decree, and we dispatch the host of heaven to execute it. So be it. Amen.

Use this as a legal instrument: read it aloud, sign it corporately, and file it in your record. Expect paperwork in the spirit; confirmations, signs, and angelic attestations.

Closing Note

Zion in session is not spectacle; it is sovereignty re-entering the world. The ekklesia's dignity is legal, not merely devotional. Learn the forms. Honour the process. Expect the angels to move like bailiffs and the books to open like court dockets. The nations wait not for louder worship but for wiser pleadings.

When the bench convenes and the gavel falls, heaven's government becomes earth's reality. The verdicts are final; the execution is precise; the Kingdom advances.

◆ ◆ ◆

ZION COURT LITURGY & DECREE PACK

Theme: *The True Church (Ekklesia): Government in Session*
By: *Anthony Mwangi — The BRANCH Seated in Zion*

1. The Call to Order — Opening Liturgy

Reader: The Judge of all the earth has taken His seat.
Assembly: Let every tongue be silent, and every spirit stand in awe.

Reader: The Lord has risen from His holy habitation.
Assembly: Zion is in session.

Invocation of the Seven Spirits and the Fire:

1. **Spirit of Wisdom** — Direct our words and open the seals of understanding.

2. **Spirit of Understanding** — Unfold hidden laws and balance truth with mercy.

3. **Spirit of Counsel** — Align our petitions with the will of the Judge.

4. **Spirit of Might** — Enforce Your verdicts and silence opposition.

5. **Spirit of Knowledge** — Record the truth and preserve the record.

6. **Spirit of the Fear of the LORD** — Guard this court with reverence and awe.

7. **Spirit of the LORD (Holy Spirit)** — Preside as Governor and Interpreter of the Throne.

8. **Spirit of Judgment and Burning** — Purify the atmosphere, cleanse the altars, and establish righteousness by fire.

Reader: The gavel has struck; the Court of Zion is in session.
Assembly: Amen. Let fire go before Him, and let His throne be established in justice.

2. Case Filing — Petition of the Saints

Case Title: _____

Petitioners: _____

Scriptural Precedent: _____

Summary of Case:

Evidence and Testimony:

Desired Verdict (Decree):

Date Filed: _____ Filed in Zion by:

_____

> *"If we confess our case before Him, He is faithful and just..."*
> *(1 John 1:9 – judicial mercy clause)*

3. Witness Record Sheet

> *"This day are ye My witnesses, saith the LORD." — Isaiah 43:10*

Case Name: _____
Verdict Rendered: _____
Date of Execution: _____
Prophetic Fulfillment / Evidence:

Recorded by (angelic officer): _____

4. Corporate Decree Template

Decree No. ____ / Year of Zion: ____
Issued by the Ekklesia in Session

By the authority of the Name above every name,
We, the assembly of the Firstborn written in heaven, standing upon the blood of the covenant and seated with Christ in heavenly places, do hereby decree:

1. That the will of the Father is established in this matter.

2. That all contrary verdicts of darkness are null and void.

3. That angels of execution are released to perform the Word of the King.

4. That this decree be sealed in heaven and manifested on earth, effective immediately.

Signed in Zion: _____
Countersigned by: _____
Witnessed in the Spirit by: _____

> *"For where two or three are gathered in My name, there am I in the midst of them." — Matthew 18:20*

5. Angelic Dispatch Protocol — Fire Seal Edition

> *"The court sat, and the books were opened." — Daniel 7:10*

Once the verdict is declared, say aloud:

> *"We seal this case in the Name of the Judge, the Lawgiver, and the King.*
> *Let every angel assigned take their charge.*
> *Let the word run swiftly and perform it."*

Then speak the Fire Clause:

> *"Spirit of Judgment and Burning, move through every word spoken.*

Consume corruption, expose deception, and sanctify the outcome.
Let no unclean spirit tamper with the record.
Let fire hedge the verdict until its full performance."

Follow with thanksgiving:

"Bless the LORD, ye His angels, that excel in strength, that do His commandments, hearkening unto the voice of His word." — Psalm 103:20

End of Session Formula:

Reader: The court of Zion is adjourned.
Assembly: The Kingdom stands. The Word reigns. Amen.

6. Closing Benediction — The Psalm 82 Fire Decree

Reader: God standeth in the congregation of the mighty; He judgeth among the gods.
Assembly: Arise, O God, judge the earth: for Thou shalt inherit all nations.

Final Declaration:

We are His court, His voice, His government in the earth.
We decree righteousness in our gates, judgment in our borders, and mercy upon our land.
Spirit of Judgment and Burning, seal every decree, cleanse every altar, and guard every word with fire.
Zion stands. The Judge reigns. The case is closed.

CHAPTER 6

The Law of Decree and Dominion

"Thou shalt also decree a thing, and it shall be established unto thee: and the light shall shine upon thy ways." —Job 22:28

I. The Power of Prophetic Legislation

*T*he Law of Decree and Dominion are not a religious act of speaking words into the air; it is spiritual legislation issued from the throne of divine government. Every true decree is born from communion, not emotion; from alignment, not ambition. In the heavenly courts, words are not noise; they are *law*. The Ekklesia's calling is to legislate heaven's constitution upon earth (**Matthew 6:10**). Dominion, therefore, begins where revelation becomes decree and decree becomes law.

When a word is released by a spirit under authority, it becomes a **living edict** in the unseen realm; angels respond, creation adjusts, and systems bow. But when a word is spoken without legal standing, it is void of governmental power.

Prophetic legislation demands:

1. **Position** — seated with Christ (*Ephesians 2:6*)

2. **Purity** — clean lips before the altar (*Isaiah 6:7*)

3. **Protocol** — alignment with the written and spoken Word

Only such decrees can pierce the atmosphere with judicial light.

II. The Seal of the Spirit on Spoken Words

The Holy Spirit is Heaven's **seal and notary** in the courtroom of creation. He authenticates what the Father wills, and the Son speaks. When believers speak under His unction, He stamps that word with legality.

In this seal, the Spirit operates as:

- **The Breath of Witness** — confirming truth in heaven and earth (*John 15:26*)

- **The Fire of Authentication** — burning away false speech and igniting true decrees (*Jeremiah 23:29*)

- **The Oil of Continuity** — ensuring that divine decrees endure across generations

Thus, the Spirit's seal turns mere utterance into spiritual governance. A true decree carries **fire, oil, and breath;** the three witnesses of divine approval.

III. The Authority of Binding and Loosing (Matthew 16:19)

> *"And I will give unto thee the keys of the kingdom of heaven: and whatsoever thou shalt bind on earth shall be bound in heaven..."*

Christ's statement to Peter was not about exorcism alone; it was a **constitutional transfer of judicial power**.

1. Binding — The Restraint of Illegality

To bind (*deo* in Greek) is to forbid, arrest, or hold unlawful that which heaven has not permitted. It is the legal act of silencing spiritual or natural rebellion by divine precedent. When the Ekklesia binds, it enforces heaven's verdict.

2. Loosing — The Release of Legal Freedom

To loose (*luo*) is to untie what has been unjustly held. It restores liberty, inheritance, or revelation. To loose in the Spirit is to open sealed gates and release divine potential locked by ignorance or demonic decree.

These two actions, binding and loosing, form the **core mechanisms of dominion**. Through them, the Church legislates heavenly justice upon earthly systems.

IV. Courtroom Cases of Abraham, Moses, and Elijah

Every prophet stood in the **Court of Heaven** not as a spectator, but as a legal voice representing divine justice. Each case reveals principles of decree and dominion.

1. Abraham — The Court of Intercession (Genesis 18)

Abraham stood before God to negotiate for Sodom. His petitions were not emotional prayers but *legal arguments*.

- **Spiritology:** He appealed to God's nature as Judge of all the earth.

- **Soulogy:** He reasoned with compassion aligned to divine mercy.

- **Theology:** He invoked the covenant promise that made him lawful to stand.

Thus, his decrees carried *judicial empathy* — truth joined with mercy.

2. Moses — The Court of Covenant (Exodus 32–33)

When Israel sinned, Moses interceded using the covenant of Abraham as a legal foundation. He said, *"Remember Abraham, Isaac, and Israel."*
He reminded heaven of its own constitution. This is the model of legal intercession; not pleading from fear, but reasoning from covenant memory.

3. Elijah — The Court of Verdict (1 Kings 17–18)

Elijah declared drought and rain not by chance, but by divine verdict. He stood before the Throne (*"As the Lord liveth, before whom I stand"*). His decree carried immediate execution because it aligned with the heavenly case file against Baal.
In him, the power of the spoken word became elemental dominion.

V. The Spirit of Judgment and Burning: The Legal Fire of Dominion

Before a decree can stand, it must pass through fire. The *Spirit of Judgment and Burning* (**Isaiah 4:4**) purges the lips of the intercessor so that the decree becomes pure flame. This Spirit:

- Judges the motive before judging the matter.

- Burns away the chaff of emotion and error.

- Converts speech into *lawful light.*

Without this purification, the tongue becomes a weapon of rebellion. But under the fire, it becomes a **rod of righteousness** — a sceptre in the mouth (**Isaiah 11:4**).

VI. The Seven-Dimensional Revelation of the Law of Decree

and Dominion

Dimension	Meaning	Manifestation in the Decree
Spiritology	The Breath of God legislates creation	The Spirit utters through the believer's inner man — decrees as divine breath
Soulogy	The renewed mind becomes the courtroom	Conscience and intellect align with divine justice — decree flows from judgment, not impulse
Physiology	The tongue as an instrument of power	Nervous and vocal systems sanctified — physical sound becomes spiritual vibration
Theology	Christ the Word as the constitution	Every decree must root in the Logos, not human will — the Word is the supreme law
Chronology	Decree precedes dominion	Order: revelation → decree → establishment → dominion
Typology	Abraham, Moses, and Elijah as legislative	Intercession (Abraham), Covenant remembrance (Moses), Prophetic verdict (Elijah)

	archetypes	
Technology	Voice as spiritual technology	Sound waves transmit legal energy — decree travels through dimensions and reforms systems

VII. The Courtroom of Light — The Legal Ecosystem of Heaven

In the heavenly court, the Throne is flanked by the seven Spirits of God; each Spirit is a *legal office* of divine operation. When the Spirit of Wisdom drafts, the Spirit of Understanding interprets; when the Spirit of Counsel argues, the Spirit of Might executes; when the Spirit of Knowledge documents, the Spirit of Fear enforces, becoming the two streams of the spirit of Judgment and burning, which is the Spirit of the Lord presiding as Judge.

The believer who decrees within this ecosystem participates in heaven's government. His words become **lawful sounds**, carrying judicial resonance.

VIII. The Dominion Protocol — How to Decree Lawfully

1. **Ascend** — Enter through worship and purity of heart.

2. **Receive Verdict** — Listen for the Word proceeding from the Throne.

3. **Decree** — Speak only what the Spirit confirms.

4. **Seal** — Apply the Blood and the Spirit's witness.

5. **Execute** — Act in obedience to what was decreed.

This is the **Dominion Circuit** — from revelation to manifestation.

IX. The Prophetic Court Decree

"O Zion, stand in the court of the King.
Let your tongue become a rod of fire,
Your mouth a gavel of righteousness.
Every illegal decree spoken against you, be annulled!
Every lawful word of destiny, be sealed by the Spirit!
For the law shall go forth out of Zion,
And the Word of the Lord from Jerusalem."

X. Summary: The Law That Births Dominion

The **Law of Decree** is not noise; it is the release of divine justice through spiritual consciousness. Dominion begins when believers stop *pleading* and start *legislating*.

Speech becomes sceptre; revelation becomes constitution; alignment becomes enthronement.

Thus, the Ekklesia rises as heaven's living parliament; voices of fire seated in Zion, speaking as one with the King.

CHAPTER 7

Thrones, Crowns, and Sceptres

"And hast made us unto our God kings and priests: and we shall reign on the earth." — Revelation 5:10

I. The Order of Kings and Priests

*H*eaven's government is not monarchical in isolation but royal-priestly in order. Dominion without priesthood becomes tyranny; priesthood without dominion becomes religion. Christ embodies both the Lion and the Lamb, King and Priest, Sceptre and Altar.

The Ekklesia inherits that dual order. Every believer is summoned to **rule as a king** and **minister as a priest**. The altar is our courtroom, and the throne is our jurisdiction.

- **Priestly Order (Intercession):** brings heaven down through incense and sacrifice.

- **Kingly Order (Legislation):** extends heaven outward through decrees and dominion.

When these merge, Zion becomes a functioning government, not just a worship gathering but a spiritual parliament.

"Ye are a royal priesthood..." (1 Peter 2:9) — royal speaks of authority; priesthood of access.

The true Church — the *Ekklesia of Christ* — was never meant to be a congregation of worshippers only, but a **governmental body of kings and priests (*Revelation 1:6; 5:10*)**. This order is the restoration of Eden's dominion mandate: *to reign with God, not merely to serve before Him.*

The Ekklesia's power lies not in performance but position: **standing in the courts, seated on the throne, ministering at the altar — simultaneously.**

1. The Kingly Dimension — The Soul's Dominion

The kingly order operates in the **realm of decision and decree**, the sphere of the soul renewed and enthroned under the Spirit. Kings legislate through wisdom and discernment; their authority flows from righteousness, not position. The soul becomes the **seat of dominion**, mirroring the divine court where Christ sits at the right hand of God.

2. The Priestly Dimension — The Spirit's Intercession

Priests minister before the fire; kings rule from it. The priestly office sanctifies what the kingly office declares. Through the altar of intercession, the priest births the word into manifestation. The Spirit of Grace empowers the priest to cleanse atmospheres, purify motives, and align decrees to heaven's record.

3. The Melchizedek Pattern

Christ, after the order of *Melchizedek*, unites these two streams: authority and intimacy. His sceptre is righteousness; His crown is wisdom; His throne is the heart purified by fire. The Ekklesia inherits this dual mantle to *reign by revelation and serve by fire.*

II. The Typology of Crowns in Scripture

Crowns are not mere ornaments; they are **spiritual endowments** in Scripture mark a *dimension of victory,* authority, *and inheritance.* Crowns are not ornaments; they are visible tokens of **spiritual jurisdiction.** Each crown reveals a dimension of dominion within the believer's transformation into the image of Christ. The Greek word *stephanos* means *a wreath of reward or authority bestowed after conquest.*

1. **The Crown of Life** — *Endurance through trial (James 1:12)*
   Granted to those who endure testing and overcome temptation. Spiritologically, it represents victory over mortality, when the soul yields fully to the Spirit of Life.

   • Spiritology: Crown of breath — Spirit's victory over death.

   • Typology: The breath restored in Adam through Christ.

2. **The Incorruptible Crown** — *Self-mastery (1 Corinthians 9:25)*
   Awarded to those who discipline the body and master desire. Physiologically, it reflects divine control over the nervous and hormonal systems; the temple is fully sanctified for divine government.

   • Soulogy: Mastery over desires and thoughts; dominion within.

   • Typology: The disciplined mind as the inner throne of peace.

3. **The Crown of Righteousness** — *Faithfulness in waiting (2 Timothy 4:8)*

This is the seal of legal justification in the heavenly courtroom; the verdict of divine approval over a life aligned with God's statutes. It is the robe of judgment made visible.

- Theology: Established by justification, maintained by alignment.

- Typology: Judicial crown — sign of lawful standing.

3. The Crown of Glory — *Service and stewardship (1 Peter 5:4)*

Given to shepherds and mature sons. It radiates the Spirit of Wisdom and Glory, the visible shining of the inner anointing that governs nations.

- Physiology: Manifested through service, visible through the body's works.

- Typology: Glory made flesh — the body as vessel of majesty.

4. The Crown of Rejoicing — *Harvest of souls (1 Thessalonians 2:19)*

Seen on the elders around the throne, symbolising the perfected intellect submitted to divine consciousness; thought purified into light.

- Chronology: Fruit-bearing through time; joy as proof of dominion.

- Typology: The crown of multiplication — dominion expanding through influence.

Each crown corresponds to a **throne of function** representing not status, but *stature;* the internal configuration of the spirit, soul, and body under the reign of the Spirit of Wisdom.
Crowns are not decorations for heaven; they are **seals of responsibility** for reigning with Christ in time and eternity.

"Let no man take thy crown" (**Revelation 3:11**) is a warning not against theft, but forfeiture of spiritual authority through compromise.

III. Sceptres as Symbols of Government and Light

The **sceptre** (Hebrew: *shebet*, meaning rod, tribe, authority) is the emblem of divine kingship and lineage. It is the **Word in motion**, the spoken decree that carries the lightning of divine justice. The **sceptre** is not a rod of decoration but of direction. It represents the *extension of the King's will*. In the spiritual realm, a sceptre is light made lawful — revelation turned to rule.

> • **Psalm 45:6:** "Thy throne, O God, is for ever and ever: the sceptre of thy kingdom is a right sceptre."

> • The sceptre is righteousness embodied — a straight, unwavering beam.

When Christ rules with a "rod of iron," it is not cruelty but incorruptibility — the immovable line of divine order.

Iron in Scripture speaks of endurance, unbending truth.

In prophetic typology:

> • **Moses' Rod** — Judicial power over creation.

> • **Aaron's Rod** — Priestly power of resurrection (it budded).

> • **The Rod of Christ's Mouth** (*Isaiah 11:4*) — Prophetic power of decree.

Each sceptre, then, represents a dimension of light:

1. **Judicial Light** — to govern circumstances.

2. **Priestly Light** — to restore what has died.

3. **Prophetic Light** — to speak new order into being.

Every decree of the Ekklesia flows through one of these rods, depending on the nature of the case.

1. The Word as Sceptre

When Christ speaks, His word proceeds as a rod of iron (*Revelation 19:15*). This rod disciplines the nations and subdues rebellion in both spirit and flesh. Every prophetic decree, spoken in righteousness, extends the sceptre of His reign.

2. The Tribe as Sceptre

Genesis 49:10 declares, *"The scepter shall not depart from Judah."* Judah — the tribe of praise — carries the judicial authority of the Spirit. Praise is not music; it is **legislative sound** that shifts thrones and governments.

3. The Sceptre of Light

Psalm 45:6–7 reveals the mystery of illumination in dominion: *"The sceptre of Thy kingdom is a right sceptre... therefore God hath anointed Thee with the oil of gladness."*
Light is the evidence of righteous government; when the inner lamp burns with holy oil, decrees manifest in glory.

The tongue of the righteous is a sceptre when it speaks from revelation.

IV. How the Ekklesia Rules through Righteousness

True dominion is never about dominance — True government is not political; it is *spiritual jurisdiction rooted in right alignment* and manifestation of divine justice through mercy. *Righteousness is relational order made visible.*

The Ekklesia rules not by force but by **alignment**. Wherever heaven's order is mirrored and earth's obedience, authority flows naturally.

Righteousness is heaven's constitution; every other law derives from it.

- **Spiritology:** Righteousness is the frequency of divine breath.

- **Soulogy:** It is peace in the conscience.

- **Physiology:** It is health and equilibrium in the body.

- **Theology:** It is conformity to Christ.

- **Chronology:** It is time redeemed.

- **Typology:** It is Melchizedek — King of Righteousness.

- **Technology:** It is the operational code of heaven's systems.

Thus, the Ekklesia legislates by living. Our obedience becomes ordinance; our worship becomes law.

1. Courtroom of the Conscience

Within every believer is a courtroom where truth and deceit contend. When the Spirit of Judgment and Burning enter, the conscience becomes the throne of God's verdict. From this inner Zion, decrees flow outward to subdue the world.

2. The Sceptre of the Mouth

The believer's tongue becomes the sceptre when yielded to the Spirit. *"He shall smite the earth with the rod of His mouth"* (**Isaiah 11:4**). Each spoken word becomes legislation when backed by righteousness and divine order.

3. The Crowned Mind

When the mind is renewed, the will is enthroned. This is dominion by *thought in light*. The crowned mind no longer reacts to darkness but governs it by understanding.

4. Thrones as Dimensions of Dominion

Each believer matures through ascending thrones:

- **Throne of Faith** — authority over fear.

- **Throne of Wisdom** — government of understanding.

- **Throne of Glory** — manifestation of divine nature.
  These thrones exist within, forming the architecture of Zion's government in man.

When the saints walk in righteousness:

- Thrones activate in the spirit realm.

- Crowns begin to shine (recognition of divine ownership).

- Sceptres emit light (governmental execution).

This is why Isaiah prophesied, *"The work of righteousness shall be peace; and the effect of righteousness quietness and assurance for ever."* (**Isaiah 32:17**)

Where righteousness rules, chaos bows.

V. The Seven-Dimensional Revelation of Thrones, Crowns, and Sceptres

Dimension	Revelation	Operation in Dominion
Spiritology	The Spirit enthrones Christ within man	Inner communion creates external authority
Soulogy	The renewed mind wears the crown of thought	Alignment of reason to truth brings judgment and clarity
Physiology	The body bears visible glory through	The physical realm mirrors internal dominion

	obedience	
Theology	Christ as King-Priest — the pattern	His order defines the legitimacy of all spiritual rule
Chronology	Seasons of enthronement follow seasons of testing	Crowns appear after proven endurance
Typology	David (throne), Esther (sceptre), Joseph (crown)	Archetypes of intercessory governance
Technology	Light as data of the government	Decrees transmitted as luminous codes through words, gestures, and prophetic actions

VI. Thrones and the Governmental Map of Heaven

In the heavenly vision, the throne of God stands amidst the sea of glass; lightning issues forth, and elders cast their crowns before Him. This act is not surrender, but *alignment*: they acknowledge that all dominion flows from the Lamb.

When the Ekklesia mirrors this act on earth, casting crowns of self-will and raising sceptres of righteousness, heaven's government manifests through them. The Spirit of Judgment and Burning passes through the congregation, refining every throne until only light remains.

Every throne in heaven is a **seat of principle** — not furniture but frequency. Thrones vibrate at the resonance of righteousness.

- **Father's Throne:** Source of all order.

- **Son's Throne:** Mediation of justice through mercy.

- **Spirit's Throne:** Distribution of divine power through the Ekklesia.

Beneath these lie the **thrones of the elders**, symbolic of perfected governance — 24 seats representing eternal administration. When the Ekklesia aligns, it joins this celestial parliament.

Every local assembly is meant to mirror one of these seats; a throne of light governing a territory by decree, intercession, and righteous conduct.

VII. Prophetic Typology of Royal Dominion

Figure	Crown / Sceptre Symbolism	Prophetic Meaning
David	Crown from Judah	Worship enthrones government
Esther	Golden sceptre	Intercession gains access to power
Solomon	Throne of ivory and gold	Wisdom structures peace

Joseph	Crown of Pharaoh	Servanthood becomes rule
Melchize dek	King of Righteousnes s	Fusion of priesthood and kingship
Christ	Many crowns (*Revelation 19:12*)	Dominion perfected and multiplied in His body

These are not ancient relics but spiritual technologies — *patterns encoded in time* that reappear wherever righteousness reigns.

VIII. The Spirit of Judgment and Burning — The Fire Behind the Crown

Every crown is forged in fire. The Spirit of Judgment and Burning is heaven's refiner's furnace. Before a throne is granted, a fire must test the metal.

- **Judgment** removes false motives.

- **Burning** seals the heart in holiness.

A believer who escapes fire will never carry true authority. The more intense the purification, the heavier the crown.

In prophetic order:

No crown without cross, no sceptre without surrender, no throne without trial.

IX. The Royal Decree of Zion

"The Lord shall send the rod of Thy strength out of Zion:
rule Thou in the midst of Thine enemies." — Psalm 110:2

The rod (sceptre) emerges from Zion — the Ekklesia in her governmental identity. Dominion is not aggression; it is influence born of presence.

When the saints decree, they do not beg; they legislate. The throne speaks through them. Their crowns sparkle in the unseen; their sceptres blaze like lightnings.

Thus, Zion's kings and priests restore balance between heaven and earth. Every word they speak becomes architecture; every act of worship, a constitutional clause.

Prophetic Decree

"O Zion, rise and sit in judgment!
Let every false crown fall, and every true sceptre shine.
Let the Spirit of Wisdom rest upon your brow,
And the rod of your mouth decree righteousness.
The government shall be upon your shoulders,
And the kingdoms of this world shall become the
kingdoms of our Lord and of His Christ."

X. Summary: Reigning through Righteousness

Thrones establish order.
Crowns validate identity.
Sceptres execute authority.

Together they form the **architecture of divine governance** within and around the Ekklesia.

The true Church rules not from pulpits, but from presence, not through personality, but purity. Her power is the righteousness of Christ; her weapon is decree; her crown is glory; her sceptre is light.

When this government fully awakens, the kingdoms of this world will know:

"The Lord reigneth; let the earth rejoice." (Psalm 97:1)

CHAPTER 8

The Governmental Prayer

"For out of Zion shall go forth the law, and the word of the Lord from Jerusalem." — Isaiah 2:3

Overview

Governmental prayer is not petition; it is participation in the rulership of Christ. It is not begging Heaven to move; it is Heaven moving through man. It is the Ekklesia standing in its judicial posture to legislate, ratify, and enforce the decrees of the Throne.

When one prays from Zion, one speaks from within the Mountain of God, not from the valley of need. Such prayer is throne-talk, law-speech, and covenant enforcement, because Zion is the spiritual seat of divine government on Earth.

1. Praying from Zion, Not to Zion

Spiritology Dimension

Zion is not a geographical hill; it is the spiritual summit of divine indwelling; the mountain of the Spirit in the heart of man. The

Holy Spirit enthrones Christ within the believer, turning the inner man into the "holy mountain" (*Ezekiel 28:14*). From this elevation, the believer speaks *as* Zion, not *to* Zion.

Soulogy Dimension

To pray from Zion requires the soul to ascend. It is not emotional desperation, but alignment; a soul in agreement with the Spirit. When the mind, will, and emotions are yielded to divine law, prayer shifts from reaction to legislation.

Physiology Dimension

Even the body participates. The tongue becomes the sceptre, the lungs the throne-room wind, and the breath the incense that rises before God. The act of breathing becomes priestly, each exhalation a declaration of government.

Theology Dimension

Zion-prayer mirrors the prayer of Christ: "Thy kingdom come, Thy will be done." It is Christ interceding through His body (*Romans 8:26–27*). When the Church prays from Zion, she echoes His voice, and Heaven recognises the sound of its King.

Typology Dimension

Moses ascended Sinai; Elijah ascended Carmel; Jesus ascended the Mount of Transfiguration; all prefiguring the believer's spiritual ascent into Zion. Every true intercessor prays from the mountain, not the plains.

Chronology Dimension

Governmental prayer matures through the ages; from the patriarchal altars, to David's psalms, to Christ's blood, to the final Zion in Revelation, where the Lamb and His bride reign together.

Technology Dimension

Tongues, decrees, and prophetic utterances function as divine frequencies; Heaven's legal sound-waves that alter realities. When believers pray from Zion, they transmit the "frequency of kingship," causing atmospheres to obey.

2. Spiritual Protocols of Courtroom Intercession

Governmental prayer operates by order, not zeal. The heavenly court is structured, with ranks and roles.

- **Protocol 1 — Approach:** Enter by the Blood (*Hebrews 10:19*). The Blood is the access code.

- **Protocol 2 — Reverence:** Stand in awe before the Judge of all. This posture aligns the heart to justice.

- **Protocol 3 — Evidence:** Bring the Word, not emotion. The Scripture is the legal constitution.

- **Protocol 4 — Witness:** The Spirit bears witness with your spirit (*Romans 8:16*). Agreement with Him seals the verdict.

- **Protocol 5 — Enforcement:** Angels are sent forth to perform the word (*Psalm 103:20*).

In Zion, the intercessor is not a beggar but a legal officer. Petition turns to legislation; supplication becomes execution.

3. Verdicts, Appeals, and Witness Testimony

Verdicts: When a case is decided in Heaven, it is sealed by the decree of the Word and executed by the Spirit. Every verdict corresponds to divine justice, written before time (*Daniel 7:10*).

Appeals: When injustice persists on Earth, the Ekklesia does not complain; it reappeals to the Throne. Elijah's prayer for rain was an appeal for restoration of covenant order (*1 Kings 18*).

Witness Testimony:

- The **Blood of Christ** testifies of mercy.

- The **Word** testifies of the truth.

- The **Spirit** testifies of power.

These three bear record in Heaven (*1 John 5:7*). The intercessor joins their testimony on Earth, forming a quorum of divine agreement; Heaven cannot deny its own witnesses.

4. The Blood of Jesus as Final Evidence

The highest evidence in the Courtroom of Heaven is not human plea but divine blood.
The Blood speaks better things than Abel (*Hebrews 12:24*); it silences accusation, cancels handwriting, and seals eternal justification. When the Ekklesia presents the Blood, every demonic prosecutor loses jurisdiction.

Through the Blood:

- **Verdict of righteousness** is pronounced (*Romans 5:9*).

- **Authority of kingship** is restored (*Revelation 1:5–6*).

- **Covenant of peace** is enacted (*Colossians 1:20*).

Thus, the governmental prayer ends not with "Amen" but with **"It is finished."**
Because in Zion, intercession is not merely prayer; it is participation in the eternal judgment of the Lamb.

The Seven-Dimensional Summary of Governmental Prayer

Dimension	Expression	Function
Spiritology	Breath of God through man	Creates spiritual authority
Soulogy	Agreement of will with divine	Establishes inner alignment

	law	
Physiology	Voice and breath as instruments	Manifests decree through sound
Theology	Christ interceding through His Body	Connects prayer to divine order
Chronology	Fulfilment of the eternal plan	Joins past covenants to present action
Typology	Zion as mountain of legislation	Symbolises divine jurisdiction
Technology	Tongues and decrees as frequencies	Executes spiritual verdicts in time and space

Prophetic Declaration

"O Lord, let the sound of Zion rise in me.
Make my breath an instrument of law.
Let the Spirit of burning cleanse my altar,
That I may decree only what is written.
As I pray from Zion, let Heaven's verdict echo through
my being, and let the kingdoms of this world become the

kingdoms of our Lord and of His Christ."

PART III

THE BLUEPRINT OF THE KINGDOM

CHAPTER 9

The 7-Dimensional Ekklesia

"Wisdom hath builded her house, she hath hewn out her seven pillars." — Proverbs 9:1

Overview

*T*he Ekklesia is not a religious assembly; it is the spiritual architecture of Heaven manifested on Earth, a living organism governed by the sevenfold Spirit of God. Every dimension of its existence reflects one aspect of divine administration, forming the perfect pattern of Kingdom order.

The 7-Dimensional Ekklesia reveals how the Spirit, Soul, and Body of Christ cooperate with the divine constitution to express God's government in all spheres: spiritual, moral, physical, historical, symbolic, and technological. It is the *blueprint* by which the invisible Kingdom becomes visible.

I. Spiritology — The Breath and Blueprint of Construction

"Except the Lord build the house, they labour in vain that build it." — Psalm 127:1

The Ekklesia begins where the Spirit begins: in breath, not in brick.

Spiritology reveals the **inner current of divine life** that forms the invisible structure of all things. The Holy Spirit is both **Architect** and **Executor**, shaping each member as a living stone fitted by revelation, not religion.

- **The Breath as Blueprint:** Each decree of God is a living code written in Spirit. When spoken, it becomes structure.

- **Sevenfold Building:** The Seven Spirits (*Isaiah 11:2*) form the seven pillars — *Wisdom, Understanding, Counsel, Might, Knowledge, Fear of the Lord that stream to the Spirit of Judgement and burning resulting in Holiness.*

- **Governance Flow:** The Spirit builds from the inside out; indwelling the heart, enlightening the mind, then governing the body.

- **Purpose:** To make the Ekklesia a breathing temple; animated by divine wind, ruled by inner light, and moved by spiritual synchronisation.

II. Soulogy — The Mind as Throne of Governance

"Be ye transformed by the renewing of your mind..." — Romans 12:2

The soul is the seat where divine revelation becomes human consciousness. When renewed, it turns into a **throne of government:** able to perceive, judge, and legislate in alignment with the Spirit.

- **The Soul's Three Courts:** *Mind* (Judicial Reason), *Will* (Legislative Power), *Emotion* (Executive Flow).

- **Alignment Protocol:** Spirit writes → Soul interprets → Body enacts.

- **Righteous Dominion:** The soul governs emotion through truth, not feeling; governs decision through covenant, not impulse.

- **Zion's Mind:** The soul of Christ in His people becomes the mind of Zion; an intelligent city of divine consciousness.

III. Physiology — The Body as the Living Temple

> *"Know ye not that your bodies are the temples of the Holy Ghost?" — 1 Corinthians 6:19*

The Ekklesia's government is not abstract; it is incarnational. The body is the visible house where divine administration touches creation.
Every part of the body mirrors a priestly function:

- **The Heart** — the *Altar* of continual fire.

- **The Brain** — the *Ark* of divine thought.

- **The Tongue** — the *Sceptre* of decree.

- **The Hands** — the *Doors* of execution.

- **The Feet** — the *Pillars* of Dominion.

Thus, physiology reveals how God reigns *through* the body. When the body becomes obedient to the Word, it transforms into a government, a physical outpost of the invisible Kingdom.

IV. Theology — The Constitution of Divine Order

"For the Lord is our judge, the Lord is our lawgiver, the Lord is our king; he will save us." — Isaiah 33:22

Theology in the 7-Dimensional Ekklesia is not abstract doctrine; it is **constitutional revelation**. It defines how the Godhead governs creation.

- **The Father** — *Judge and Source of Law.*

- **The Son** — *King and Word made Flesh.*

- **The Spirit** — *Executor and Enforcer of Verdicts.*

This threefold order — *Judicial, Royal, and Prophetic* — flows through the Body of Christ, forming the structure of true Ekklesia government.

Therefore, theology is the legal language of Heaven — every truth becomes legislation, every precept becomes jurisdiction, every doctrine becomes divine law in motion.

V. Chronology — The Timeline of Kingdom Manifestation

"A day with the Lord is as a thousand years, and a thousand years as one day." — 2 Peter 3:8

Chronology shows how the Ekklesia unfolds through time, not as a single event, but as an ongoing revelation.

- **From Adam to Christ:** The *shadow of the house* was built (temples, altars, tribes).

- **From Christ to Pentecost:** The *foundation of the house* was laid — the Spirit descended.

- **From Pentecost to Zion's Revelation:** The *completion of the house* — the Bride perfected, the Spirit enthroned.

Each millennium carries one pillar of the Sevenfold Spirit. We are in the **Seventh Day**, the *Sabbath Age*, when the Ekklesia becomes the dwelling place of God fully — the House of Rest.

VI. Typology — Patterns, Shadows, and Thrones

> *"See that thou make all things according to the pattern shewed thee in the mount." — Hebrews 8:5*

Typology decodes divine architecture. The Ekklesia is patterned after the heavenly Zion.

- **Moses' Tabernacle** — shows the *procession of access.*

- **David's Tabernacle** — reveals *worship and rulership united.*

- **Solomon's Temple** — manifests *wisdom and glory established.*

- **Christ's Body** — becomes *the final living structure.*

Every type unveils how God reigns in man; from altar to throne, from shadow to substance, from pattern to presence.

VII. Technology — The Operation of Word, Sound, and Spirit

> *"The entrance of thy words giveth light." — Psalm 119:130*

Technology in the Ekklesia refers to the **spiritual mechanisms** by which revelation is transmitted, encoded, and manifested.
God speaks in *three modes*: **Vision, Written, and Spoken.**

- **Vision** — The dimension of the *Spirit* (revelation).

- **Written** — The dimension of the *Soul* (codification).

- **Spoken** — The dimension of the *Body* (manifestation).

Each mode carries spiritual technology, how the divine blueprint becomes tangible reality. The Spirit illuminates; the mind interprets; the mouth executes.

This is the operation of prophetic technology: Heaven's architecture built by sound and light.

The Seven Spirits as the Seven Thrones of Administration

Each Spirit of God corresponds to a throne within the Ekklesia's government:

Spirit of God	Throne Function	Kingdom Expression
Spirit of Wisdom	Design & Construction	Builds the pattern
Spirit of Understanding	Insight & Structure	Establishes interpretation
Spirit of Counsel	Guidance & Strategy	Directs governance
Spirit of Might	Power & Enforcement	Executes decrees
Spirit of Knowledge	Revelation & Light	Illuminates mysteries

Spirit of the Fear of the LORD	Sanctification & Reverence	Keeps order and holiness
Spirit of Judgment and Burning	Purification & Completion	Perfects, refines, and enthrones

This final Spirit is **the sealing fire.**
Where Wisdom begins by building, *Judgment and Burning* ends by refining.
It removes mixture from motive, pride from power, and impurity from purpose, until the Ekklesia itself becomes fire that cannot be quenched.

It is the **Spirit of Final Witness**, the courtroom fire that tests every structure and reveals the gold within.
It dwells, not visits; consuming dross yet preserving essence, ensuring that what remains is eternal.

Thus, the Seven Spirits are not merely attributes — they are the *seven thrones* of divine governance, the inner parliament of Heaven within the believer.

Blueprint Summary Table — The 7-Dimensional Ekklesia

Dimension	Nature	Function in the Ekklesia	Outcome
Spiritology	Breath and Revelation	Gives divine life and order	Foundation of identity
Soulogy	Mind and Will	Translates revelation into	Inner government

		law	
Physiology	Body and Action	Manifests divine structure	Visible dominion
Theology	Constitution and Law	Defines Kingdom order	Doctrinal government
Chronology	Time and Fulfilment	Unfolds divine history	Prophetic timing
Typology	Pattern and Prophecy	Encodes spiritual meanings	Wisdom of structure
Technology	Sound and Light	Operates revelation	Manifestation of reality

Prophetic Declaration — The Dwelling Fire of the Ekklesia

O Eternal Spirit, breathe once more through the stones of Your house.
Build again by Wisdom, align by Understanding, and counsel by Your hidden voice.
Strengthen every gate with Might; fill every lamp with Knowledge.
Let the Fear of the LORD return as the atmosphere of Zion

where hearts bow, and voices tremble before truth.

And now, O Spirit of Judgment and Burning,
dwell among us as consuming order and living fire.
Burn away the dust of religion, the smoke of ambition,
the strange incense of self-glory.
Refine the gold, preserve the pattern, seal the covenant.

Let the Ekklesia be fire-built, not man-made
a temple of light, a throne of flame,
where the Word rules, and the Spirit dwells.
From Wisdom to Burning, from Breath to Glory,
let Your government rest upon our shoulders
until the whole earth mirrors Zion,
and the House of Fire becomes the City of the King.

CHAPTER 10

Patterns of Government in Scripture

"That which hath been is now; and that which is to be hath already been." — Ecclesiastes 3:15

Overview

*T*he government of God is not new; it is eternal.
Every covenant, altar, and throne from Genesis to Revelation is a pattern revealing one unbroken principle: God reigns through divine order, not human structure.

From **Eden's communion** to **Zion's glory**, the Spirit traces a continuous line of governance; not of hierarchy, but of harmony. The Ekklesia, in her end-time fullness, is the mature expression of that same order, where Spirit and man rule as one.

This chapter unveils that progression, *from Eden to the New Jerusalem*, as a living continuum of divine government, refined through priestly, kingly, and prophetic prototypes.

I. Eden — The First Administration of Dominion

"And the Lord God took the man, and put him into the garden of Eden to dress it and to keep it." — Genesis 2:15

Eden was more than a garden; it was the **first governmental domain.**

Adam was the prototype *governor-priest*, embodying heaven's rule on earth.

- **The Throne:** God's presence walking in the cool (Spirit's atmosphere).

- **The Law:** The Word spoken "Of every tree thou mayest freely eat..."

- **The Court:** The Tree of Life (divine verdict), the Tree of Knowledge (testing of law).

Eden's order was maintained by **obedience through intimacy; dominion without domination.**

When Adam broke divine alignment, he didn't lose religion; he lost *governmental access.* The curse was jurisdictional, not emotional; the loss of throne-rights on earth.

Redemption, therefore, is not only forgiveness; it's **restoration of rulership** through union with the Spirit.

II. Melchizedek — The Prototype of Priest-King Dominion

"He was the priest of the most high God. And he blessed him..." — Genesis 14:18–20

Melchizedek appears as a mysterious embodiment of divine governance; **priesthood and kingship fused in one.**

He held no lineage, no written law, yet carried *everlasting authority.* His bread and wine foreshadowed communion:

government sustained by covenant.

In him, the pattern emerges:

- **King of Salem** — Order of Peace (righteous rule).

- **Priest of God Most High** — Order of Intercession (spiritual mediation).

- **Blessing Abraham** — Order of Transfer (authority through covenant).

The Melchizedek Order is the unbroken line of heavenly administration, fulfilled in Christ and extended through His Ekklesia.

It is the pattern where **altar and throne unite**, where spiritual governance flows through fellowship, not force.

III. Moses — The Pattern of Law and Mediation

"See that thou make all things according to the pattern shewed thee in the mount." — Exodus 25:40

Moses introduced *constitutional government,* the written law that mirrors divine order. The tabernacle, priesthood, and statutes became visible expressions of heavenly protocol.

- **Spiritology:** The cloud and fire — God's presence as witness.

- **Soulogy:** The law written on tablets — revelation becoming thought.

- **Physiology:** The tabernacle — the human body in symbolic form.

Each tribe, each gate, each altar reflected a court system in divine order:

Priests (intercessors), Levites (servants), Elders (governors),

Prophets (legislators).

Moses' model revealed that *government is worship structured as law.*

The mountain (Sinai) was the courtroom; the ark was the throne; the blood was the signature.

In Christ, the written becomes living; the **Word made flesh**, re-establishing government as grace fulfilled, not abolished.

IV. David — The Pattern of Throne and Worship

> *"And I will set up thy seed after thee... and I will establish the throne of his kingdom for ever."* — *2 Samuel 7:12–13*

David's reign was the meeting point of law, worship, and warfare, **the musical throne of divine government.**
Every psalm was a decree; every harp-string a line of legislation. Where Moses legislated in words, David legislated in worship.

- **The Tabernacle of David** was open, without veil; the first prophetic type of the New Covenant order.

- **Zion** became the governmental centre, not of military, but of music and prophecy.

- **The Throne of David** became the prophetic seat Christ would inherit (*Isaiah 9:6–7*).

David restored what Adam lost: rulership through relationship. He governed through *presence*, not politics. In him, the Ekklesia sees its mirror: a people crowned with praise, ruling by revelation, establishing peace through the sound of righteousness.

V. The Early Church — Apostolic Order Restored

"And God hath set some in the church, first apostles, secondarily prophets, thirdly teachers..." — *1 Corinthians 12:28*

The early Ekklesia was structured around divine government, not human charisma.

- **Apostles** carried foundational authority; builders of law and order.

- **Prophets** served as the divine interpreters; the voice of the court.

- **Teachers** codified revelation; doctrine as constitution.

- **Evangelists and Pastors** enforced and nurtured the decrees of the Kingdom.

Their gatherings were not religious meetings but **councils of heaven on earth**.
Prayer was legislative. Worship was jurisdictional. The breaking of bread was a covenantal ratification.

Their pattern: *Acts 15* — the Jerusalem Council, where the apostolic decree decided doctrine.
Every act flowed from heaven's verdict, confirming that *true government in the Church is prophetic legislation by the Spirit of Truth.*

VI. The End-Time Ekklesia — The Prophecy of Micah 4:1–2

"In the last days it shall come to pass, that the mountain of the house of the Lord shall be established in the top of the mountains..."

Micah foresaw a time when Zion's government would rise above

81

all earthly systems; not by conquest, but by *truth enthroned.*

- **"The mountain of the house of the LORD"** — The perfected Ekklesia, the dwelling of divine government.

- **"Established in the top of the mountains"** — Spiritual supremacy, the reign of the Spirit above human dominion.

- **"People shall flow unto it"** — Nations drawn not by fear, but by the weight of righteousness.

- **"For out of Zion shall go forth the law..."** — Heavenly verdicts legislated through the Spirit-filled Church.

This prophecy unveils the **final restoration of Eden's order**: Man once again ruling creation through communion; heaven and earth merged in one voice; Christ's throne manifested in a corporate body.

It is the return of **governmental worship**, the re-emergence of divine civilisation, when the Spirit of Judgment and Burning refines the nations into one Kingdom under one King.

7-Dimensional Breakdown of Governmental Patterns

Dimension	Expression in History	Purpose
Spiritology	God's presence in Eden and Zion	Establish divine habitation
Soulology	Renewal of thought in Moses' law and David's psalms	Form the inner government
Physiology	Tabernacle, Temple, Body of Christ	Manifest heavenly order on earth

Theology	Covenants and priesthoods	Define the structure of divine law
Chronolog y	From Adam to the New Jerusalem	Reveal the maturing stages of government
Typology	Patterns: Melchizedek, Moses, David	Encode prophetic blueprints
Technology	Word, worship, sound, and Spirit	Transmit and enforce divine decrees

Prophetic Reflection

"The throne has never left the earth; only the awareness of it faded.
From Eden's breath to Zion's fire, the same government continues; unseen by the natural eye, but witnessed in every covenant, in every prophet who built by the pattern.
Now, the Spirit calls the Ekklesia to remember the design, to become again the place where Heaven governs through man."

CHAPTER 11

The Technology of the Spirit

"For the Spirit searcheth all things, yea, the deep things of God." — 1 Corinthians 2:10

I. The Architecture of Divine Intelligence (Spiritology)

*T*he Technology of the Spirit is not mechanical; it is organismic, alive, and self-revealing. The Holy Spirit is the intelligence of divine order; the invisible circuitry that connects heaven's will to earthly manifestation. Every spiritual law, decree, and revelation travels through the network of the Spirit, much like lightning from the throne (Ezekiel 1:13–14).

- The Spirit is not merely power: He is *patterned intelligence.*

- Every prophetic word carries a design code that aligns with the Lamb's Book of Life.

- Revelation, therefore, is the language of construction; when God speaks, He builds.

   In Zion, technology is not invention; it is **divine synchronisation**. The Spirit does not invent new truths; He reveals ancient order hidden in eternity.

II. The Intelligence of the Soul (Soulogy)

The soul acts as the **processor** of revelation. When the Spirit downloads divine truth, the soul interprets, frames, and manifests it through thought, imagination, and speech.

- Revelation becomes transformation when the soul yields to divine rhythm.

- Prophets and intercessors serve as translators between frequencies: spiritual language and human understanding.

- The mind renewed by the Spirit becomes a *holy processor* of heavenly technology.
  Thus, the **Spirit reveals**, the **soul interprets**, and the **body executes**, forming a triune circuit of divine operation.

III. The Physiology of Prophetic Technology (Physiology)

Just as electricity flows through circuits, the **anointing flows through vessels**. The body is wired with divine pathways: neural, vocal, and sensory — which the Spirit activates for revelation and decree.

- The tongue becomes a *pen of fire* (**Psalm 45:1**).

- The heart functions as the *altar processor:* where revelation is judged, purified, and released.

- Hands transmit virtue (**Mark 5:30**), eyes transmit discernment, and breath carries decree.
  When sanctified, the body becomes an interface between the seen and unseen; a living tabernacle where the Word becomes visible through motion, voice, and embodiment.

IV. The Law of Revelation, Interpretation, and Execution

(Theology)

Every move of God follows a **threefold technological law**:

1. **Revelation** — The Spirit unveils divine intent (*Amos 3:7*).

2. **Interpretation** — The soul aligns perception to divine meaning.

3. **Execution** — The body enacts the will of God on earth. This triune operation mirrors the Godhead itself:

   • The Father **wills**,

   • The Son **interprets**,

   • The Spirit **executes**.

When the Church operates in this trinitarian rhythm, she becomes *the technology of heaven on earth*. This is why Jesus said, "As the Father hath sent Me, so send I you" (*John 20:21*) — a statement of **spiritual deployment**.

V. The Timeline of Prophetic Technologies (Chronology)

From Eden to Revelation, God's technological systems evolve as revelation matures:

• **Eden** — the interface of *presence technology* (God walked with man).

• **Moses** — the *law tablet system*, the first "download" of divine code.

• **David** — *sound technology* through psalms, worship, and prophetic frequency.

• **Christ** — the *incarnate Word*, the perfect integration of heaven and earth.

• **Pentecost** — *fire technology*, the Spirit's descent to distribute divine power across many bodies.

- **Zion (the end-time Church)** — the *fusion of all technologies*: light, sound, word, and breath, operating through an awakened body in perfect unity with the throne.

VI. Typology of Thrones, Scrolls, and Seals (Typology)

The Spirit's networks are governed by divine instruments:

- **Thrones** — represent *domains of authority*. Every revelation sits upon a throne of purpose.

- **Scrolls** — represent *records of mandate*. Every decree aligns with a written law in heaven.

- **Seals** — represent *dimensions of confidentiality*. Only maturity can break a seal (*Revelation 5:1–9*).

When John wept because no man could open the scroll, it was not weakness; it was recognition that divine technology requires *a worthy interface*. Christ, the Lamb, became that interface, proving that revelation flows only through obedience unto death.

VII. Technological Expression of the Word (Technology Dimension)

The Technology of the Spirit manifests through **three communication modes:** *Vision, Written, and Spoken*:

1. **Vision** — The Spirit projects divine imagery into consciousness.

2. **Written** — Revelation is encoded into Scripture and scrolls for preservation.

3. **Spoken** — The prophetic mouth becomes a sound-portal that releases decrees.

Every true decree is a *download of divine intelligence;* not merely words, but sound-waves encoded with Spirit-life. When believers decree from Zion, they broadcast from heavenly servers of light, influencing systems, nations, and timelines.

VIII. The Spirit of Judgment and Burning: The Power Core of Heaven's Technology

All divine technology operates by **purity and fire.**
The *Spirit of Judgment and Burning* (**Isaiah 4:4**) is the cleansing force that maintains the integrity of revelation.

- Judgment ensures order.

- Burning ensures purity.
  Together, they prevent corruption of divine code, purging pride, ambition, and false prophecy from the vessel.

Thus, the power grid of heaven is not electricity; it is **holiness.** Only the sanctified can sustain the voltage of revelation.

IX. The Manifestation of the Ekklesia as a Living Network

The mature Church is no longer a building; she is a **living operating system of the Spirit**, synchronised across nations, altars, and timelines. Each believer becomes a **spiritual device**, connected to the throne's central intelligence. When united in decree and worship, the global Body forms the *Heavenly Internet of Zion,* transmitting divine verdicts across creation.

X. Summary Revelation

The Technology of the Spirit is the administration of divine order through living vessels.
It is the unseen circuitry that connects heaven and earth through holiness, light, and obedience.
In Zion, every saint becomes a transmitter of divine law, every

prayer a code of justice, and every decree a manifestation of God's government.

PART IV

THE ECCLESIA IN THE LAST DAYS

CHAPTER 12

The War of Thrones

"And there was war in heaven: Michael and his angels fought against the dragon." — Revelation 12:7

I. The Cosmic Conflict of Thrones (Spiritology)

*T*he War of Thrones is not a war of weapons, but of words, altars, and covenants. It is the ultimate confrontation between two spirits: the Spirit of Truth and the Spirit of Whoredom (Hosea 4:12). One proceeds from the Throne of God; the other from the Mystery of Babylon.

In this war, thrones represent spiritual governments of consciousness; each throne ruling from a different atmosphere.

- **Zion's Throne** manifests in purity, order, and law.

- **Babylon's Throne** operates in confusion, mixture, and seduction.
  The Holy Spirit, as the *Spirit of Judgment and Burning*, exposes these counterfeit systems, cleansing the Ekklesia of all strange fire and aligning her back to divine protocol.

Every war in Scripture, from Eden to Revelation, is a continuation of the **Throne War**: who shall rule creation, truth or deception, Spirit or flesh?

II. Babylon vs. Zion — The Counterfeit Church (Soulogy)

Babylon is the *fallen soul system;* the collective consciousness of man exalting self above God.

- It is the church that **worships the gifts above the Giver**.

- It builds towers of influence without foundations of holiness.

- It trades in revelation without transformation.

In contrast, **Zion is the sanctified soul,** the bride who carries the mind of Christ and the government of righteousness.

- Her worship is judicial.

- Her songs are decrees.

- Her priests are flames of fire.

Thus, the War of Thrones is fought in the *mind of the Church:* Babylon seeks to corrupt the imagination, while Zion sanctifies it into prophetic sight. The battle for the Bride begins in the heart and is won through sanctified perception.

III. The Physiology of Rebellion and Holiness (Physiology)

In the human vessel, Babylon manifests as spiritual disease; rebellion in the bloodstream, pride in the heart, and lust in the eyes.
But Zion manifests as divine alignment; a body whose members are instruments of righteousness.

- **The heart** becomes the altar of government.

- **The tongue** becomes the sceptre of decree.

- **The hands** become the implements of intercession.
Thus, the body becomes a living temple in which **Zion reigns** or **Babylon usurps**. Every believer carries within them both a temple and a tower; one must fall for the other to rise.

IV. The Theology of Thrones (Theology)

The War of Thrones reveals God as **Judge**, **King**, and **Husband**.

- As **Judge**, He exposes the injustice of Babylon.

- As **King**, He restores dominion to His saints.

- As **Husband**, He purifies His Bride through covenant fire.

This is the theology of judgment and intimacy: Zion's government is born out of the **Spirit of Judgment and Burning** (*Isaiah 4:4*). Every act of divine judgment is actually an act of divine love, cleansing the Bride so she can share His throne (*Revelation 3:21*).

Babylon, on the other hand, is built on **fornication with kings of the earth;** the union of religion with corruption, spirituality with ambition. Its theology is sensual, soulish, and self-serving. Zion's theology is covenantal, fiery, and holy; a union that produces sons, not slaves.

V. Chronology — From Babel to Babylon to the Beast (Chronology)

The pattern of Babylon unfolds through time:

- **Babel** (*Genesis 11*) — the first counterfeit unity built without the Spirit.

- **Babylon** (*Daniel 1–5*) — the empire of idolatry and

domination.

- **Mystery Babylon** (*Revelation 17–18*) — the end-time religious–economic system opposing the Kingdom.

Each stage represents the evolution of human rebellion: from language to government to worship. The spirit behind them all is **Lucifer's ambition**: to ascend the throne of the Most High.

But at the end of the age, Zion arises; the city of God, the government of righteousness. Her citizens are priests of fire, her foundations are judgments, and her King is the Lamb.

The last war is not fought in nations first, but in altars; between holy fire and strange fire.

VI. Typology — Babylon the Harlot vs. Zion the Bride (Typology)

In typology:

- **Babylon** is the *Harlot Woman* — clothed in luxury, drunk on the blood of saints, seated on seven mountains of corrupted power.

- **Zion** is the *Virgin Bride* — clothed in fine linen, washed by the Word, and seated beside her King.

Babylon's crown is **gold mixed with filth**, but Zion's crown is **purity refined by fire**.

The harlot rides the beast; the bride reigns with the Lamb.

Thus, every woman in Scripture: Eve, Jezebel, Mary, and the New Jerusalem, represents a spiritual system of **union and reproduction**. The question is: *What seed do you carry?*

Babylon conceives rebellion; Zion gives birth to redemption.

VII. The Technology of Thrones and Verdicts (Technology)

Heaven's throne operates by divine **technology of decree**:

- Every throne emits sound frequencies (*Revelation 4:5*).

- Every verdict is sealed by blood and executed by angels.

- Every altar connects to a courtroom in heaven.

Babylon's technology is counterfeit: witchcraft, manipulation, false prophecy: using *soulish energy* to counterfeit divine power. But Zion's technology flows through **the Spirit of Judgment and Burning**, ensuring that every decree proceeds from holiness, not ambition.

When the Ekklesia prays from Zion, their decrees carry divine voltage; judgments become legislative fire, and their words reorder nations.

VIII. The Spirit of Whoredom vs. the Spirit of Truth

The **Spirit of Whoredom** trades intimacy for influence. It causes ministries to prostitute their anointing, to sell revelation for applause, and to replace the Bridegroom with the marketplace.

But the **Spirit of Truth** restores covenant fidelity, returning worship to purity and ministry to holiness.

This is the Spirit that washes the Bride, aligning her emotions, desires, and motives to the Lamb.

Whereas Babylon manipulates, Zion intercedes.

Whereas Babylon seduces, Zion sanctifies.

Whereas Babylon sells truth, Zion becomes truth.

XI. The Bride Emerging from Corruption

The Bride's emergence from Babylon is a **prophetic exodus**. She is called to "come out of her, My people" (*Revelation 18:4*). This exodus is not physical but spiritual; a detachment from polluted altars, false alliances, and soulish patterns.

- Her garments are washed in fire.

- Her mind is renewed by light.

• Her worship becomes a judicial decree.

This is the *restoration of the true Church*: not a denomination but a habitation; a body built upon the Lamb, judged by fire, and governed by righteousness. She is the manifestation of Zion in the earth: the woman clothed with the sun, crowned with twelve stars, standing upon the moon of dominion (***Revelation 12:1***).

X. Summary Revelation

The War of Thrones is the final separation between holy fire and strange fire, between the Bride and the Harlot.
Babylon represents corrupted worship; Zion represents sanctified government.
The Spirit of Judgment and Burning is cleansing the Ekklesia, so that the throne of the Lamb may be established in every heart.
When the Bride fully emerges, every counterfeit throne shall fall; and the kingdoms of this world shall become the Kingdom of our Lord and of His Christ.

CHAPTER 13

The Rise of the Overcomers

"And he that overcometh, and keepeth My works unto the end, to him will I give power over the nations." — Revelation 2:26

I. The Remnant as Judicial Ambassadors (Spiritology)

*T*he overcomers are not a religious elite: they are judicial ambassadors, raised by the Spirit to represent Heaven's government in a fallen world. Each carries the seal of the Lamb and the fire of the Throne within.

Their identity is not measured by visibility but by *spiritual jurisdiction*. They legislate quietly from prayer rooms, from hearts that burn in hidden chambers, until the decrees echo through nations.

To overcome is not merely to survive temptation, but to **subdue atmospheres;** to bring the rebellious structures of soul and system back into obedience to the King.

The Spirit of **Judgment and Burning** marks these ambassadors. It purges their motives until righteousness becomes instinct. Their presence judges darkness without words; their silence convicts realms.

They are born of Zion, not of Babylon, and they know that true authority flows only through alignment, not ambition.

They do not shout to prove power. They decree because they've died.

II. The Government of Overcomers (Soulogy)

In *Revelation 2–3*, Christ speaks to seven churches; seven conditions of the soul within the Body.
Each promise to "him that overcometh" reveals a throne, a sceptre, and a dimension of rulership:

- **Ephesus:** The throne of *first love* — government by devotion.

- **Smyrna:** The throne of *endurance* — government by faith under pressure.

- **Pergamos:** The throne of *truth* — government by sword against compromise.

- **Thyatira:** The throne of *purity* — government by holiness amidst corruption.

- **Sardis:** The throne of *watchfulness* — government by discernment over death.

- **Philadelphia:** The throne of *faithfulness* — government by covenant loyalty.

- **Laodicea:** The throne of *intimacy* — the seat beside the King Himself.

Each stage is a courtroom training; the soul purified, tested, and crowned.

The overcomer's soul becomes Zion's chamber where divine law and human will are reconciled.

III. The Spirit of Might and Dominion (Physiology)

Might is not muscle; it is spiritual voltage. It flows through obedience.

When the Spirit of Might rests upon a vessel, their words carry mass; weight in the unseen. It is this Spirit that made Samson tear lions, David subdue kingdoms, and Elijah shut the heavens. But in the Ekklesia, this Might no longer expresses through physical battle, but through the physiology of **faith under fire**.

- **Hands** become extensions of divine justice.

- **Feet** become instruments of dominion.

- **Hearts** become engines of decree.

The Spirit of Might is the energy of divine kingship flowing through human vessels. It empowers the body to perform what the Word commands, turning prophecy into action and prayer into law.

Dominion is not noise; it is the quiet authority of alignment.

IV. Thrones of Judgment Given to the Saints (Theology)

Daniel 7:27 declares:

> *"The kingdom and dominion... shall be given to the people of the saints of the most High."*

This is the legal transfer of government from the fallen principalities back to the redeemed body. The saints do not sit beside the throne; they *share it.*

Theologically, this is the fulfilment of *Genesis 1:26* — "Let us make man in Our image... and let them have dominion."
Man was created to be a judicial image of God on earth, reflecting divine law into creation. The fall corrupted that rulership; the Cross restored it; and the Spirit enforces it.

In the end-time courtroom, Christ does not rule alone: He rules **through** His Body, the overcomers.
They sit as co-judges, co-heirs, co-reigners; executing verdicts that flow from His mouth.

V. Chronology of Dominion — From Adam to the Overcomer (Chronology)

The story of dominion follows this divine timeline:

- **Adam:** Lost the throne through disobedience.

- **Abraham:** Recovered jurisdiction by faith.

- **David:** Modelled kingship through worship.

- **Christ:** Restored full government through the Cross.

- **The Ekklesia:** Executes the verdict as the Body of the King.

- **The Overcomers:** Manifest the kingdom in final judgment and reign.

Each age advances the legal restoration of God's rule on earth. Dominion has always been about **trust;** whether the creature can bear the Creator's authority without corruption.
The overcomers are the final proof that redeemed man can.

VI. Typology — Thrones in Flesh and Fire (Typology)

Every overcomer mirrors a biblical prototype:

- **Enoch:** Dominion through intimacy.

- **Joseph:** Dominion through wisdom and forgiveness.

- **Esther:** Dominion through intercession.

- **Daniel:** Dominion through purity under empire.

- **John the Beloved:** Dominion through revelation.

Each represents a different throne of the Spirit, all converging in the Body of Christ. Together they form the Council of Zion, a living pattern of governance distributed among many members yet unified by one Spirit.

In this council, love is law, and judgment is mercy burning with purity.

VII. The Technology of Dominion (Technology)

Heaven's government operates through divine *technologies of rule*:

- **Scrolls** contain the decrees.

- **Seals** authorise execution.

- **Sceptres** transmit authority.

- **Crowns** identify jurisdiction.

Overcomers learn how to operate these technologies: not through rituals, but through relationship. The Spirit teaches them how to speak heaven's language, how to synchronise voice and vibration with divine will.

When they decree, it is not opinion; it is resonance with the Throne.

Their technology is alignment; their tools are obedience.

The true technology of dominion is a yielded tongue.

VIII. The Final Order — The Reign of the Saints

When the thrones of judgment are set (*Daniel 7:9–10*), the overcomers will not be spectators; they will sit in session.
Their robes are not ornamental; they are legal garments woven from obedience and faith. Their crowns are not decoration; they are signets of trust.

The Ekklesia becomes the living court where God dwells in man to judge creation through righteousness.
This is the fulfilment of *Psalm 149:9*; "To execute upon them the judgment written: this honor have all His saints."

Dominion returns home.
The kingship of man becomes the mirror of God's justice.
The overcomers reign, not because they demanded thrones, but because they carried crosses until the Cross became a Throne.

Prophetic Summary

The rise of the overcomers marks the transfer of spiritual government.
They are the sons refined by the Spirit of Judgment and Burning, tested in secret, enthroned in light.
Through them, Zion's rule fills the earth.
They are the living verdict of Heaven; the final witness that Christ's reign is absolute and eternal.

CHAPTER 14

The Nations Before the Court

"Let the nations be judged in Thy sight. Put them in fear, O LORD, that the nations may know themselves to be but men." — Psalm 9:19–20

I. The Judgment of Nations Through the Ekklesia (Spiritology)

The Ekklesia is not only a spiritual house; it is Heaven's international court seated upon the earth.

When Christ said, "Go ye therefore, and teach all nations" (Matthew 28:19), He was not sending missionaries: He was sending governors, empowered to enforce divine law across the borders of culture and empire.

Judgment of nations does not begin with earthquakes and famine; it begins when the Spirit of Judgment and Burning dwells among the righteous, cleansing the altar of intercession. From that place, divine decrees move like lightning through the unseen, shaking foundations of systems, thrones, and ideologies.

The Ekklesia judges not by hate but by *alignment*.
Each decree, prayer, and intercession becomes a **verdict** that either invites mercy or activates correction.
Where Babylon enthrones rebellion, Zion enthrones righteousness; until every nation must choose whom it will serve.

The Spirit-filled Church is not waiting for judgment; she *is* the instrument of judgment, sanctified by the blood to legislate mercy and truth in balance.

II. Apostolic Witnesses and Prophetic Diplomacy (Soulogy)

The apostles and prophets are Heaven's diplomats; witnesses who stand between mercy and wrath. Their soul is trained to hold paradox without compromise: love for the lost and loyalty to the Throne.
In divine diplomacy, they represent Christ to nations not merely in word, but in *nature*. Their meekness disarms kings; their purity convicts governments.

- The **apostolic witness** establishes law — building cities upon truth.

- The **prophetic diplomat** interprets law — revealing the mind of the Spirit in time.

Together they carry the dual identity of the Lamb and the Lion: humility in approach, fire in decree.
Through them, Heaven conducts its foreign affairs, summoning nations to repentance, peace, or reform.

When ambassadors of Zion speak, it is not politics; it is *prophetic litigation*, an invitation for nations to enter divine order before harsher judgments awaken them.

III. The "Rod of Iron" and the Rule of Righteousness

(Physiology + Theology)

The rod of iron in *Revelation 19:15* symbolises **incorruptible governance;** the kind that cannot bend under pressure or compromise under favour.
Christ wields this rod, but He extends it through His Body: the overcomers. Each believer's body becomes a **conduit of righteous enforcement** when fully surrendered to the Spirit.

- The **hand** represents the execution of justice.

- The **mouth** declares the sentence.

- The **feet** tread upon iniquitous ground.

- The **heart** holds the mercy seat, ensuring judgment flows from love, not pride.

Theologically, righteousness is not a moral code; it is *the alignment of all created order to the Throne.*
When the rod moves through decree, it corrects distortion in systems, economies, and institutions.
Wherever truth is spoken under the anointing of the Spirit of Judgment and Burning, invisible rods of light strike corruption until repentance or removal occurs.

The rod of iron is not brutality; it is divine stability made manifest through uncompromised saints.

IV. The Call to Legislate for the Harvest (Chronology + Typology)

Before Christ's return, the Ekklesia enters her final role: **to legislate for the harvest.**
This is the courtroom age where intercession and government merge. The Spirit calls the Body to draft heavenly decrees that prepare the nations for redemption, not destruction.

Throughout history, every move of harvest was preceded by a

decree from Heaven:

- Noah's ark — judgment for cleansing and preservation.

- Moses before Pharaoh — decree of deliverance and separation.

- Elijah on Carmel — decree of fire and decision.

- The apostles at Pentecost — decree of the Spirit and expansion.

Now, in the age of consummation, the Ekklesia once again stands before the Court.

The Spirit beckons watchmen, judges, and intercessors to legislate not for comfort but **for the alignment of harvest fields**. Every soul reaped must pass through righteous gates, and those gates are established by decrees.

Revival without legislation becomes chaos; legislation without compassion becomes tyranny. The Spirit seeks both.

V. The Nations in Court (Chronology)

Revelation 20:12 reveals the ultimate tribunal:

> *"And I saw the dead, small and great, stand before God; and the books were opened."*

That courtroom scene is not postponed for eternity; it begins now whenever the Spirit convenes intercessors to open scrolls and read charges over regions.

Each nation is already on trial, not for ethnicity, but for obedience.

Heaven measures them by how they treat truth, justice, and the witness of the saints within their borders.

- Some nations are found wanting because they silenced prophets.

- Others are weighed and found light because they rejected mercy.

- Yet a remnant of nations will bow, becoming sheep nations under the Shepherd-King.

Zion's decrees tilt the balance. The Ekklesia's verdicts shape history until the courtroom shifts from intercession to manifestation; when Christ appears as the Judge, all verdicts have foretold.

VI. Technology of National Legislation (Technology Dimension)

Heaven's legislation moves through precise spiritual technologies:

- **Scrolls** — contain the statutes of mercy and judgment.

- **Altars** — serve as points of upload where intercessors release decrees into time.

- **Thrones** — authorise the jurisdiction of those decrees.

- **Winds** — carry enforcement through angelic networks.

When the Ekklesia gathers in true unity, they become an **international data centre** for divine justice. Decrees are not mere prayers; they are legal files transmitted into global spiritual systems.
As each saint aligns with the Spirit of Judgment and Burning, their collective voice generates the sound of Zion, a thunderous legislation that awakens nations.

VII. Prophetic Summary — When Government Becomes Harvest

The judgment of nations is not vengeance; it is preparation.
The Court of Heaven is not designed to condemn but to *purify for governance.*
When the Ekklesia legislates, the Spirit releases both fire and rain — judgment to cleanse, and grace to restore.

- Babylon falls, but harvest rises.

- Thrones shake, but truth stands.

- Governments collapse, but Kingdoms are born.

The nations are not spectators in this story — they are participants before the Court.
The Ekklesia does not curse them — she calls them to order.
For the rod of iron is tempered by the heart of the Lamb,
and every decree aims at one end: **the redemption of creation through righteous rule.**

CHAPTER 15

The Reign of the Lamb and the Bride

(The Sabbath Reign — The Union Of Dominion And Rest)

I. Spiritology — The Wedding as Enthronement

*I*n the Spirit, the wedding of the Lamb is not merely a celebration; it is enthronement. It is the divine moment when union becomes government. The Lamb, slain yet enthroned, marries His Bride not for romance but for reign. The Spirit of Judgment and Burning prepares the Bride, purging every trace of Babylon's mixture until she is transparent; a city of pure gold like clear glass (Revelation 21:18).

This marriage is the *Spirit's coronation* within man. The Holy Spirit, as the oil of consecration, seals the Bride into governmental sonship; "the Spirit and the Bride say, Come" (**Revelation 22:17**). The Spirit who hovered in Genesis now dwells within the perfected Bride, completing the circle of creation: from Eden's betrothal to Zion's eternal marriage.

To be wed to the Lamb is to sit where He sits; in judgment, in glory, and in rest. The Spirit of the Bride is the Spirit of Sabbath, where all dominion flows from love's throne.

II. Soulogy — The City, the Temple, and the Bride

The soul of the redeemed ekklesia is threefold: **city**, **temple**, and **bride;** each revealing a phase of divine indwelling.

- **As City:** The redeemed mind becomes Jerusalem, structured with order and righteousness. Every gate is a revelation, and every foundation a name; the twelve apostles as the eternal constitution of truth.

- **As Temple:** The heart becomes the dwelling of divine glory. The Lamb is the Lamp — not an external source but the *internal consciousness of light*. The Bride's emotions become incense, her desires priestly, and her will aligned with the will of the King.

- **As Bride:** The will of man is fully yielded to the will of Christ; "Thy will be done on earth as in heaven." The soul is no longer independent; it has become covenantal. The Bride's submission is her crown; her purity is her throne.

Thus, the soul becomes governmental; no longer tossed by feelings but governed by covenant.

III. Physiology — The Body as the Resting Throne

The body is the *holy city made visible*. It is the land where the Spirit dwells bodily (*Colossians 2:9–10*). Every redeemed cell is a living stone; every organ participates in worship. The body of the Bride is not a temple of effort but of **rest;** the Sabbath embodied.

When the Spirit fully reigns in the body, disease bows, corruption ceases, and the flesh becomes fireproof — glorified.

The *Throne of the Lamb* is the divine DNA enthroned in man, and the *river of life* flows from within the body as living waters. The physical form becomes the geography of God's rest: Zion clothed in flesh.

IV. Theology — Revelation 21–22 as the Final Government of Light

Revelation 21–22 is not the end; it is the **constitution of eternity**. It unveils the ultimate theocracy where God and the Lamb are the Temple, and the nations walk in their light. Every decree now proceeds from love, not law; from intimacy, not distance.

This is the **final Sabbath**, when all government flows from rest. There are no more altars of sacrifice; only the *altar of light*, where every decree is a radiance of glory. The Lamb's throne in the city signifies that divine government and divine relationship are inseparable. Theology reaches its fulfilment: God dwelling with man, and man reigning with God.

V. Chronology — From Eden to New Jerusalem

- **Eden:** Betrothal — the Spirit walking with man.

- **Abraham:** Covenant — the promise of divine inheritance.

- **David:** Kingship — the prophetic pattern of throne and worship.

- **Christ:** Marriage — the union of heaven and earth in the Word made flesh.

- **Pentecost:** Indwelling — the Holy Spirit as the seal of the Bride.

- **New Jerusalem:** Reign — eternal Sabbath where all time enters rest.

Time is not ending; it is *being completed*. The seventh day becomes eternal, the Sabbath becomes the city, and the city becomes the Bride.

VI. Typology — The Bride, the City, and the Sabbath

- **Eve** — the first Bride drawn from Adam's side — prefigures the Church born from Christ's pierced side.

- **Ruth** — the redeemed gentile — symbolises the Bride called out of nations to rest at the feet of her Redeemer.

- **Esther** — the intercessor-queen — typifies the ecclesia legislating from the king's court.

- **Mary** — the vessel overshadowed — embodies the Sabbath womb that births the divine Word.

Each typology reveals that true dominion begins with *rest* and manifests through *union*. The Bride is the Sabbath womb where kingship and worship are one.

VII. Technology — The Throne System of the Spirit

Heaven operates on divine technology — **Throne, Scroll, and Seal**. The *Throne* is the mind of God (intelligence), the *Scroll* is His Word (instruction), and the *Seal* is the Spirit (execution).

In the Reign of the Lamb and the Bride, this system is transferred to the Bride:

- Her mind becomes the **throne** where divine thoughts are seated.

- Her mouth becomes the **scroll**, releasing decrees as lawful sounds.

- Her spirit becomes the **seal**, authorising heaven's will on earth.

This is the *technology of rest;* decrees no longer from striving, but from union. The Bride legislates by **being** — not doing. Dominion is no longer warfare; it is radiance. Every word spoken from rest becomes *law of light.*

The Sabbath Rest of the Throne

The final government of the Lamb is the Sabbath restored. The seventh day becomes eternal dominion, not inactivity, but completion. In the city of God, work becomes worship, and worship becomes law. The throne is the altar, and the altar is rest.

> *"Blessed are they that do His commandments... that they may have right to the tree of life." (Revelation 22:14)*

The Bride reigns by rest — the ultimate dominion of the Sabbath Spirit.
The Lamb reigns through love — the government of light.
Together they form the everlasting kingdom: **Zion — the Sabbath of God.**

PART V

*THE MANIFESTO OF THE
HEAVENLY GOVERNMENT*

CHAPTER 16

The Constitution of the Ekklesia

(The Word, the Blood, and the Spirit as the Triune Seal of Dominion)

I. Spiritology — The Word as Law, the Blood as Seal, the Spirit as Witness

*T*he Ekklesia does not operate by human constitutions, creeds, or traditions; it operates by the Triune Constitution of Heaven: the Word, the Blood, and the Spirit.

- **The Word** is the **Law of Light**, the eternal decree that frames all creation (*John 1:1–3*).

- **The Blood** is the **Seal of the Covenant**, making the Word living, not legalistic (*Hebrews 9:14–15*).

- **The Spirit** is the **Witness and Executor**, ensuring that what was decreed and sealed is manifested on earth as it is in heaven (*1 John 5:8*).

These three agree as one; not in theory, but in divine function. Every law of the Kingdom flows from this living constitution.

When the Spirit writes the Word upon the heart (*Jeremiah 31:33*), the believer becomes a *living parchment*, sealed in the Blood of the Lamb.

This is the secret of divine government: the Word declares, the Blood justifies, and the Spirit enforces.

II. Soulogy — The Statutes of Love, Righteousness, and Justice

The soul is the inner court where the statutes of Heaven are internalised. The true constitution of the Ekklesia is not written on stone, but on consciousness; *the law of love*, *the standard of righteousness*, and *the measure of justice*.

- **Love** is the motive of divine law — the royal law that fulfils all commandments (*Romans 13:10*).

- **Righteousness** is the measure of divine order — the alignment of the soul to truth.

- **Justice** is the application of divine fairness — the execution of mercy in equity.

In the soul governed by these statutes, emotion becomes mercy, intellect becomes discernment, and will becomes obedience. The Bride no longer reacts to sin but legislates life. She is no longer a church of rules but a *council of righteousness*.

III. Physiology — The Body as the Temple of Law

The divine constitution does not end in the spirit or soul; it *embodies* itself. The body becomes the physical archive of heaven's law. Every cell carries a spiritual memory, and every organ functions by divine ordinance.

The *Ten Commandments*, once engraved on tablets, are now inscribed in the physiology of the redeemed.

- "Thou shalt have no other gods before Me" — written in

the **heart**, the throne of affection.

- "Thou shalt not steal" — coded in the **hands**, symbols of divine stewardship.

- "Remember the Sabbath day" — embedded in the **nervous system**, the rhythm of divine rest.

The body becomes a living constitution; a temple where *law breathes*. Thus, divine order manifests not through religious behaviour but through sanctified biology.

IV. Theology — The Ten Commandments Reinterpreted Through the Spirit

Through the Spirit of Judgment and Burning, the Ten Commandments ascend from **letter to life**:

Commandment	Spiritual Fulfilment
1. No other gods	Union with the Spirit — exclusive worship in truth
2. No graven image	Pure imagination — only the image of Christ within
3. Do not take His name in vain	Manifest His nature — the Name becomes identity
4. Keep the Sabbath holy	Dwell in rest — the Holy Spirit's indwelling
5. Honour father and mother	Honour divine origin — both natural and spiritual lineage

6. Do not kill	Preserve life — speak words that quicken, not destroy
7. Do not commit adultery	Remain faithful — covenantal purity of soul
8. Do not steal	Give freely — stewardship and kingdom generosity
9. Do not bear false witness	Speak truth — prophecy as divine testimony
10. Do not covet	Walk in contentment — dominion through gratitude

Thus, theology is no longer external morality but internal manifestation. The Spirit reinterprets law into life — every commandment becomes a *beatitude*, every ordinance becomes a *revelation of nature*.

V. Chronology — From Sinai to Zion

- **At Sinai**, the law descended as stone — external, fearful, and condemning.

- **At Calvary**, the law was fulfilled — written in blood upon wood.

- **At Pentecost**, the law was internalised — tongues of fire inscribed it on hearts.

- **At Zion**, the law is enthroned — manifesting through sons and daughters as divine governance.

This progression shows the evolution of divine constitution from external command to internal covenant. Zion represents the *final stage of law* — the Spirit fully governing creation through the Bride.

VI. Typology — The Lamb's Book as the Constitution of Eternity

In the heavenly courtroom, there are many scrolls, but one book stands above all: the **Lamb's Book of Life** (*Revelation 21:27*). It is not a ledger of names; it is the living constitution of the redeemed creation.

- **Adam** was the first draft — the prototype of divine manhood.

- **Moses** carried the written law — a shadow of the heavenly constitution.

- **Christ the Lamb** became the living Book — Word made flesh, sealed by blood.

- **The Bride** becomes the co-author — the living epistle (*2 Corinthians 3:3*).

In the Lamb's Book, names are not inked but *breathed*. Each name represents a law fulfilled, a nature perfected, a testimony sealed. The Bride's governance flows from her inclusion in this eternal text; she speaks not her will but the will of the Book.

VII. Technology — The Architecture of Divine Law

The constitution of Heaven operates on a **threefold technological architecture**:

1. **Scrolls** — contain decrees and prophetic mandates.

2. **Seals** — secure the authority of fulfilment.

3. **Thrones** — execute verdicts and judgments.

When the Lamb opens the seals, it is not the beginning of chaos; it is the activation of divine law. Each seal represents a system of heavenly governance being released into the earth realm.

The Ekklesia, as God's legislative body, operates the same way:

- **The Spirit reveals the scroll** (revelation).

- **The Blood seals the word** (sanctification).

- **The Word enthrones the decree** (manifestation).

This is how divine law becomes history — the constitution of heaven becomes the civilisation of the Kingdom.

The Eternal Constitution: Word, Blood, and Spirit

The Ekklesia is Heaven's embassy, and the Lamb's Book is its constitution. The Word defines truth; the Blood enforces righteousness; the Spirit ensures continuity. Together, they form the unbreakable seal of the Kingdom — the *Law of Life in Christ Jesus.*

> *"For the law shall go forth from Zion, and the word of the Lord from Jerusalem." — Micah 4:2*

The constitution of the Ekklesia is therefore *living, breathing, and burning* — written not with ink but with Spirit; not on parchment but in people; not for time, but for eternity.

CHAPTER 17

The Voice of the Trumpet

(The Sound of Awakening from Zion to the Nations)

I. Spiritology — The Trumpet as Breath of God

*E*very trumpet in Scripture begins as breath. Before it *is a sound, it is Spirit expelled with purpose. The word "trumpet" in Hebrew — shofar — shares root meaning with brightness and radiance. It is not just a horn but a vessel that translates divine breath into vibration.*

When the Spirit speaks through a vessel, heaven finds a mouth. The **Voice of the Trumpet** is thus the *manifestation of the Spirit's exhale through human alignment.*

It is written: "And Mount Sinai was altogether on a smoke, because the LORD descended upon it in fire, and the voice of the trumpet waxed louder and louder" (*Exodus 19:18–19*).

This growing sound is not volume; it is **progressive revelation** — breath layered upon breath, wave upon wave, until nations tremble.

The Spirit of Judgment and Burning refines that sound, ensuring no strange note proceeds from Zion. Only purified breath becomes lawful sound.

II. Soulogy — The Inner Sound of Awakening

Before a trumpet can sound in the earth, it must first sound in the soul.
Joel 2:1 says, *"Blow the trumpet in Zion, sound an alarm in my holy mountain."* Zion is not just a city; it is the *inner government of the renewed mind.*

- The **trumpet of awareness** awakens the soul from spiritual slumber.

- The **trumpet of repentance** restores divine order within.

- The **trumpet of readiness** aligns will with divine warfare.

When the soul responds to this inner call, the believer becomes both instrument and sound. The *alarm* in Zion is not fear—it is focus. It calls the mind back to dominion, summoning every fragmented thought to obedience in Christ.

The Spirit of Wisdom ensures the tone is clear; the Spirit of Understanding gives it meaning; and the Spirit of Burning sustains it in purity.

III. Physiology — The Body as a Resonating Vessel

The trumpet is fashioned from horn or metal, both symbolic of strength and resonance. Likewise, the human body is the **physical amplifier of divine sound**.

When heaven breathes, the voice must pass through flesh. Prophets trembled not from fear, but from *resonance*. The bones of Jeremiah burned with an unspoken word (*Jeremiah 20:9*). Ezekiel was lifted by sound into vision. John fell as dead when the trumpet spoke to him on Patmos (*Revelation 1:10–17*).

Our bodies are not bystanders in prophecy; they are *instruments*. The lungs carry the breath of decree, the tongue becomes the shofar of the Spirit, and the posture of the body signals submission to the Voice that speaks.

When the Ekklesia gathers, the collective body becomes a **corporate trumpet,** vibrating heaven's will into earth's systems.

IV. Theology — The Trumpet as Prophetic Order

In Scripture, trumpets define divine order:

- They **summon assemblies** (*Numbers 10:3*).

- They **signal movement** (*Numbers 10:5–6*).

- They **announce warfare** (*Joshua 6:4*).

- They **proclaim kingship** (*1 Kings 1:34*).

- They **herald judgment** (*Revelation 8–11*).

Each sound carries a theology; a revelation of divine governance through rhythm.
The seven trumpets in Revelation are not calamity; they are **legislative sounds** releasing heaven's agenda in sequence.

The Church has forgotten the language of sound. Preaching replaced *proclamation,* and worship replaced *warfare.* Yet in Zion, theology and tone are married again.
Every decree, every prayer, every praise becomes trumpet-code: *the protocol of spiritual communication in the government of God.*

V. Chronology — From Sinai to Zion to the End of the Age

- **At Sinai**, the trumpet gathered a nation under law.

- **At Jericho**, the trumpet toppled walls of resistance.

- **At Zion**, the trumpet announced kingship and covenant.

- **At Pentecost**, the trumpet became *tongues of fire*.

- **At the End of the Age**, the **last trumpet** shall sound, and incorruption will reign (*1 Corinthians 15:52*).

The prophetic line runs unbroken: every trumpet unveils another stage of divine rule. The *Voice of the Trumpet* begins as revelation and ends as resurrection; the full awakening of creation to its King.

VI. Typology — The Church as Herald and Army

The trumpet belongs to both **priests and warriors**.

- The priest blows it to declare holiness.

- The warrior sounds it to announce victory.

The Ekklesia stands as both: *a priestly army*. Her intercession sanctifies; her decree conquers.
In typology:

- **Gideon's 300** blew trumpets and broke pitchers — image of revelation breaking flesh (*Judges 7:20*).

- **Joshua's priests** marched with seven trumpets before the ark — prophetic alignment between presence and sound.

- **John the Revelator** heard the voice as a trumpet — signifying the apostolic witness of the end-time Church.

Thus, the Ekklesia becomes the *voice and vessel* — the herald that warns and the army that enforces. She is both *mouthpiece and manifestation*.

VII. Technology — The Sound Networks of Heaven

Heaven's government communicates in **frequencies**, not just phrases. Every decree has a frequency signature: a vibration of light that aligns realms.

The Spirit operates a network of *heavenly trumpets*:

- **Angelic Trumpets** — signals for movement and war.

- **Human Trumpets** — prophetic voices and assemblies.

- **Cosmic Trumpets** — celestial signs and alignments (eclipses, waves, cycles).

When these synchronise, heaven's technology releases coordinated awakening across the earth.
This is why prophecy cannot be casual; it must be **tuned**. Every prophet must discern whether their sound summons mercy or judgment, whether their tone opens gates or closes them.

In the Spirit, sound is *law in motion*. The trumpet is the tool through which revelation becomes legislation.

Final Declaration — The Sound of Government

> *Blow the trumpet in Zion. Let the sons awaken.*
> *Let every voice become a trumpet of truth.*
> *Let every decree become a vibration of justice.*
> *The nations shall hear not mere noise,*
> *but the frequency of a coming Kingdom.*

> *The Spirit of Wisdom shall shape the sound;*
> *The Spirit of Understanding shall interpret it;*
> *The Spirit of Burning shall carry it like wind through cities;*
> *Until every system bows and every power yields,*
> *to the Voice of the Trumpet*

the Voice of the Lamb enthroned in Zion.

CHAPTER 18

The Undisputed Heavyweight Government

The Final Revelation of Authority in Christ

*T*he kingdom does not emerge from the ballot box; it descends *from the Throne.*
When Christ rose from the grave, He did not rise as a priest only: He rose as the Government. His words thundered across time:

> **"All authority in heaven and in earth has been given unto Me." — Matthew 28:18**

This was not a statement of conquest; it was a coronation decree. The resurrection was the legal enthronement of the Man who bore the curse, broke it, and ascended with the keys of death and hell. In Him, dominion was no longer a lost inheritance; it was a seated reality.

To know Christ is to sit in His Government. The Holy Spirit is the Administrator of this reign; He is the very Government of God manifested within men. When He fills you, He is not merely comforting you; He is *crowning* you. The anointing is a governmental seal, not an emotional sensation.

Spiritologically: Authority flows from rest.
Soulogically: Dominion manifests when the will aligns with righteousness.
Physiologically: The body becomes the embassy of Heaven.
Theologically: Christ is the Head; the Church, His legislative Body.

The Invincible Nature of the True Church

The Church was not built to survive; it was built to *govern*.
She is not the victim of history but the throne in the midst of it.
Every storm that arises becomes the wind that lifts her higher.
The true Church cannot be defeated because she is not of this world.

> *"Upon this Rock I will build My Church; and the gates of hell shall not prevail against it."* — *Matthew 16:18*

The Rock is not Peter's personality; it is the *Revelation of Christ* that makes the Body immovable. The word "prevail" in Greek (*katischyo*) means "to overpower, to hold under siege." That means hell's gates are not attacking the Church; they are being *broken into* by it.
The Church is the aggressor in the Spirit; she advances, and hell retreats.
The gates tremble when sons stand in their seats.

When the sons of God take their positions in Zion, the invisible government of darkness collapses. Thrones, dominions, and principalities lose coherence because the true King has taken the field through His Body. The Body of Christ is the *undefeated heavyweight government;* no challenger can rise against her without falling under the weight of divine order.

The Gates of Hell and Their Defeat

Gates are legal systems, not wooden or iron structures.

They represent jurisdiction, authority, and spiritual legislation.

When Christ descended into hell, He did not sneak in; He *walked through the gates as the lawful heir.*

He stripped the adversary of his right to rule by fulfilling all righteousness.

At the Cross, every gatekeeper — Death, Hades, Leviathan, Abaddon — was rendered speechless.

The Judge had entered His own courtroom and issued the eternal verdict: **"It is finished."**

Now the Church enforces that verdict. We are not fighting for victory; we are legislating from it. The Spirit of Judgment and Burning resides in the sons who carry the fire of that final decree.

Hell's gates fall when righteousness speaks. Every altar of iniquity trembles when the sons legislate from the throne room of the Lamb.

The Coronation of the Sons of God

The final age of the Spirit is the age of *coronation.*

Creation has groaned for this unveiling; the manifestation of the mature sons who wear the diadem of dominion.

> *"The kingdom, and dominion, and the greatness of the kingdom under the whole heaven, shall be given to the people of the saints of the Most High." — Daniel 7:27*

This coronation is not ceremonial; it is judicial.

The sons receive crowns of light, not gold; authority, not ornament.

Every crown is a weight of glory, and every throne is a revelation of rest.

As they reign, they restore divine order across realms: heaven, earth, and body.

When these crowned ones stand, principalities bow; when they speak, creation obeys; when they rest, judgment flows.

They are the *undisputed government* because they rule from the place of *finished peace*.

Their warfare is worship; their decree is praise; their dominion is Sabbath.

They reign not by effort, but by enthronement.

Prophetic Summary

Dimension	Revelation of the Heavyweight Government
Spiritology	The Holy Spirit is the Government of God within man.
Soulogy	The will aligned with righteousness becomes the seat of authority.
Physiology	The body becomes the embassy and altar of divine rule.
Theology	The Kingdom is not a doctrine but a Throne.
Chronology	The seventh day (Sabbath) is the eternal reign of rest.
Typology	David's throne prefigures the Son's unshakable dominion.
Technology	Praise, decree, and judgment are spiritual

legislative tools of rule.

Prophetic Charge

Rise, O Zion, thou undivided Bride of the King.
Take your seat in the midst of the fire; let your harp decree justice, and your crown radiate peace.
The weight of your Government is not violence but glory; not sword but sound.
You are the heavyweight government of God, not because of muscle, but because of majesty.
The Throne is within you, and the Word is your sceptre.
Rule, therefore, in the midst of your enemies, and let every gate know:
The Kingdom has returned to Zion.

BONUS PART VI

THE THRONE AND THE ASSEMBLY: HEAVEN'S COURTROOM REVEALED

CHAPTER 19

The Revelation of the Throne

*B*efore there was an earth, there was a Throne.
Before there was time, there was a Seat of Eternal Judgment surrounded by fire.
This Throne is not furniture; it is the Person of the Father enthroned within His own Word.
When Ezekiel saw the fiery crystal and wheels within wheels (Ezekiel 1), he was gazing into the operating system of divine government; the Throne as the mind of God, the wheels as the processes of His will, and the fire as the Spirit of Judgment and Burning.

> **"A fiery stream issued and came forth from before Him: thousand thousands ministered unto Him, and ten thousand times ten thousand stood before Him: the judgment was set, and the books were opened." — Daniel 7:10**

This is Heaven's courtroom; not chaos, but *cosmic order*. Every word, thought, and act of man is weighed against the vibration of the Throne. The fire that proceeds from it is not anger, but purification; the light that exposes falsehood and enthrones truth.

The Assembly of Zion

When the sons are gathered in the Spirit, they are not attending a meeting; they are *entering the Assembly of Heaven.*

> *"But ye are come unto Mount Zion, and unto the city of the living God, the heavenly Jerusalem, and to an innumerable company of angels..."* — Hebrews 12:22–23

This is the Church in her true form: **the legislative body of Heaven** seated in a circle around the Lamb.
Every believer filled with the Spirit becomes part of this *heavenly senate*, where praise is motion, decree is law, and unity is jurisdiction.

In this Assembly:

- **Angels** are the witnesses.

- **The Blood** is the Advocate.

- **The Spirit** is the Recorder.

- **The Word** is the Judge.

- **The Sons** are the kings and priests co-seated with the Lamb.

The Assembly of Zion is not a democracy; it is a *theocracy of righteousness.* Here, every voice echoes the decree of the King, and every law manifests as sound. The throne speaks through the collective praise of the redeemed.

The Courtroom Protocols

To stand in Heaven's Courtroom is to align with divine order.
Every courtroom has its law, language, and atmosphere:

1. **Law — The Word of God**
   The Scriptures are not mere texts; they are *judicial statutes*.
   Every "Thus saith the Lord" carries legal weight.
   When you quote the Word, you summon the Court's jurisdiction.

2. **Language — The Blood of Christ**
   The Blood speaks better things than that of Abel (**Hebrews 12:24**). It is the eternal testimony of mercy that silences the accuser.
   The Blood does not beg; it legislates redemption.

3. **Atmosphere — Worship and Rest**
   The courtroom of Heaven is not tense but tranquil. Judgment flows from stillness, not panic.
   The Spirit of Sabbath governs all proceedings; rest is the gavel of divine justice.

In this Courtroom, intercession is advocacy, prophecy is evidence, and praise is the execution of verdicts.
When the sons rise to decree, the heavens record their words as law. What they bind on earth is bound in heaven, because their voice has merged with the Judge Himself.

The Books and the Records

Heaven's Court is built upon *scrolls*.
Every life, nation, and destiny has a record — a written pattern of divine intention.

> *"In Thy book all my members were written." — Psalm 139:16*

When the Spirit reveals your scroll, He is not predicting your future; He is summoning your original design.
Sin distorts the record, but repentance re-aligns it; prayer opens

it, and obedience fulfils it.

To walk in your book is to live in divine legality; nothing can accuse what has been written and sealed in blood.

The *Book of Life* is the registry of redeemed identities, and the *Book of Remembrance* records the words and deeds of those who fear the Lord. When these books are opened, creation aligns; when they are closed, judgment seals destinies.

The unsealing of heavenly scrolls precedes every revival on earth. Every prophetic movement is a courtroom session extended into time.

The Verdict of the Throne

The greatest verdict ever spoken was uttered on the Cross: **"It is finished."**
That was the Judge declaring His own case complete.
From that moment, all accusations lost legal ground; the only remaining power of the adversary is *ignorance.*
Satan is no longer a king; he is a *disbarred prosecutor.*

When the sons of God understand this, they stop pleading and start ruling.
They no longer ask for deliverance; they *legislate freedom.*
They do not fear judgment; they *become the embodiment of it.*

> *"Do ye not know that the saints shall judge the world?*
> *... Know ye not that we shall judge angels?" — 1*
> *Corinthians 6:2–3*

This is the final revelation of divine government: the sons are not spectators in the courtroom; they are *co-judges* in the Bench of Christ. The Spirit within them is the same Fire that proceeds from the Throne.

Spiritological Revelation

Dimension	Heavenly Courtroom Reality
Spiritology	The Throne is the Spirit's centre of government and justice.
Soulogy	The renewed mind is a witness stand where truth testifies.
Physiology	The body becomes a living ark — a seat of judgment and mercy.
Theology	The Lamb is both Judge and Justifier — justice and mercy met in Him.
Chronology	Every age is a session of divine verdict leading to the Sabbath reign.
Typology	Moses' tabernacle, David's throne, and Solomon's court prefigure the heavenly assembly.
Technology	Prayer, decree, praise, and prophetic utterance are judicial technologies of Heaven.

Prophetic Charge: The Sons in Session

O Zion, awaken; the Court is in session.
Take your seats among the witnesses; open your mouth as the pen of a ready writer.
Decree what the Spirit records; speak what the Blood testifies.
You are not on trial; you are on the throne.
The gavel of judgment is in your praise, and the fire of truth is in your breath.
Let the heavens hear the voice of the Assembly; let the earth feel the weight of divine law.
For the Throne and the Assembly are one,
and the government of God has found its resting place, in the sons seated in Zion.

CHAPTER 20

The Assembly Of Thrones: When The Body Becomes One Government

(The shift from individual Zion to corporate divine rulership — the Ekklesia as one Throne in many members.)

The Great Shift: From Personal Zion to Corporate Government

*T*here is a moment in the Spirit when personal revelation must evolve into corporate manifestation.

Zion is not just an individual seat of worship within your heart; it is a governmental body, an assembly of enthroned sons forming one organism through the Spirit of Judgment and Burning.

The Father is not raising scattered prophets, priests, and kings: He is raising a **unified assembly of thrones**.

Each believer is a throne, but together, they form **the Council of the Lamb**, a living architecture of divine order on earth.

> *"And hath made us kings and priests unto God and His Father; to Him be glory and dominion for ever and ever."*
> *— Revelation 1:6*
> *"And the thrones were set, and judgment was given to the saints..." — Daniel 7:22*

When the sons rise together in oneness of Spirit, Heaven recognises one sound — one government — one Christ.

This is not unity by human organisation; it is **unity by divine constitution**. The Blood fuses, the Word aligns, and the Spirit enthrones.

The Architecture of the Assembly

In Heaven's design, there is not one throne, but *many thrones forming one throne.*

Each son is seated in Christ, not beside Him, but **within Him**.

This forms the mystical body that governs creation: **Christ the Head, the Ekklesia His Body, the Spirit the bloodstream of governance.**

Element	Corresponding Function in the Governmental Body
Head	Christ — source of law and revelation
Heart	The Altar — where worship becomes decree
Hands	Apostolic and prophetic execution
Feet	Evangelistic dominion across the earth
Voice	The Spirit — uttering judgments and intercession
Eyes	Wisdom and Understanding — the intelligence of light

Blood	The flow of mercy and righteousness that unites all members

Thus, the Body of Christ is not an organisation; it is a **living constitution**, where every cell legislates righteousness through the flow of the Spirit.

Spiritology — The Fire of Oneness

The Spirit of Judgment and Burning is the essence of this oneness.
He burns away individuality, not identity; He purifies difference into harmony.
When the Spirit descends as fire, He does not divide men —
He **divides tongues that unite government (*Acts 2*)**.

This fire does not consume; it *orders*. It synchronises heaven and earth within the souls of men, until all function as **one throne expressing one King**.
Each decree from the corporate body then echoes with the weight of divine unanimity:

> *"Let the high praises of God be in their mouth, and a two-edged sword in their hand; to execute judgment upon the nations..." — Psalm 149:6–9*

Soulogy — The Mind of Christ as Council

The collective soul of the Ekklesia becomes the **Mind of Christ (*1 Corinthians 2:16*)**.
Individual renewal gives way to **corporate consciousness**, where believers think, feel, and decide through the same Spirit.

This is not groupthink; it is divine synchronisation.

Each soul is a council seat in the great Sanhedrin of Zion, where the Spirit of Wisdom presides.

The enemy fears not the gifted believer, but the *harmonised body*, because harmony is jurisdiction.

When souls align in truth, the court is in session; when minds agree in righteousness, Heaven decrees without delay.

Physiology — The Body as a Living Government

The body of Christ is a governmental structure in motion; bones as statutes, tendons as covenants, and blood as law enforcement.

The Spirit's administration flows through the physiology of divine order:

- **The Apostles** are the skeletal structure — they establish the frame and foundation.

- **The Prophets** are the nervous system — transmitting signals of revelation.

- **The Teachers** are the digestive system — breaking down truth into nourishment.

- **The Evangelists** are the circulatory system — spreading life through the world.

- **The Pastors** are the immune system — preserving the health of the Body.

When every system aligns, **Christ reigns bodily**, not figuratively — *He governs through physiology.*

Theology — The Many Thrones of One King

The mystery of divine government is that God enthrones Himself through His people.

The Lamb sits upon the Throne, yet shares His dominion with

143

His Bride.

> *"To him that overcometh will I grant to sit with Me in My throne, even as I also overcame..."* — *Revelation 3:21*

This is the **multi-throne mystery**:

- The Father is the Supreme Judge.

- The Son is the enthroned Word.

- The Spirit is the Power of execution.

- The Saints are the thrones of enforcement.

Thus, Heaven's government is **distributed sovereignty** — one Head, many thrones.
The Church becomes the visible expression of invisible rulership.

Chronology — The Era of the United Thrones

We are entering the **Age of the Corporate Throne**, the era when Zion matures from revelation to manifestation.
In former times, prophets bore mantles; now, bodies bear governments.

The pattern of divine order is progressive:

1. **Eden** — individual dominion.

2. **Israel** — national dominion.

3. **Church Age** — spiritual dominion.

4. **Kingdom Age (Now Emerging)** — **corporate divine dominion**: the Assembly of Thrones.

This is the season of *Daniel 7:27* fulfilled:

"And the kingdom and dominion, and the greatness of the kingdom under the whole heaven, shall be given to the people of the saints of the most High..."

The saints are no longer spectators — they are administrators of epochs.

Typology — David's Mighty Men and the United Throne

In David's reign, we see a prophetic type of the corporate throne. David did not rule alone; his throne extended through the *mighty men* who fought, judged, and executed righteousness with him.

Each was a throne; together they were the *house of David,* a shadow of the *body of Christ.*

So too, in the end-time government, the Bride does not wait for the King; she **rules beside Him.**

She carries His sceptre in her worship, His crown in her intercession, and His sword in her mouth.

This is the *Davidic order restored:* governance through harmony, worship, and justice.

Technology — The Protocols of Corporate Legislation

Heavenly government operates by spiritual technology — *Thrones in sync.*

1. **Unified Sound Technology** — When voices unite in decree, the sound frequency manifests as light (*2 Chronicles 5:13–14*).

2. **Scroll Synchronisation** — Every believer carries a scroll; when they agree, their scrolls merge into one corporate law.

3. **Seal Activation** — Obedience and holiness keep the seals

intact; rebellion breaks jurisdiction.

4. **Judgment Protocols** — Collective repentance opens the court; collective decree executes the verdict.

Through this divine technology, the Church becomes **a body of governments, not gatherings.**

The Corporate Zion Manifested

Zion is not just a mountain; it is a *system of divine governance embodied in a people.*
When the Assembly of Thrones is revealed, the earth will see a *Church that judges, heals, and reigns.*
No longer divided by denominations, they will be united by legislation; every altar aligned to the same fire, every mouth speaking the same Word.

> *"The Lord shall roar out of Zion, and utter His voice from Jerusalem; and the heavens and the earth shall shake." —Joel 3:16*

The roar is not one voice but many thrones resounding as one government.

Prophetic Declaration: The Oneness of Thrones

> *O sons of Zion, arise!*
> *You are no longer scattered stones; you are living thrones, fitly joined together in the Spirit of Judgment and Burning.*
> *You are the Assembly of Thrones, the visible government of the invisible God.*
> *Let your decrees flow as one sound; let your worship rise*

as one fire.
For the Body has become the Throne,
and the Throne has become the Body.
Christ in you is not a metaphor; it is the manifestation
of government through union.
The Lamb reigns not from afar, but from within.
And now, the kingdoms of this world become
The Kingdoms of our Lord and of His Christ
for the Body has become One Government,
and Zion has taken her seat.

CHAPTER 21

The Courtroom of Heaven and the Assembly of Thrones

(When worship becomes judgment and intercession becomes lawmaking)

The Ascension of the Ekklesia

*E*very true ascension in the Spirit leads the believer from altar to throne; from inner devotion to legislative dominion.

Prayer is not merely speech; it is appearance. When the Ekklesia gathers in Spirit and truth, it ascends to the Courtroom of Heaven, where all verdicts of creation are issued.

There, worship ceases to be performance and becomes **procedure**. The song becomes a statute, the dance a decree, the tears a signature upon the scroll.

> *"And the temple of God was opened in heaven, and there was seen in his temple the ark of his testament..."*
> — *Revelation 11:19*

The inner temple of the believer is the portal through which

Heaven's courtroom finds expression on earth.
The Spirit of Judgment and Burning presides, not to destroy, but to **refine the witnesses**.

Spiritology — The Fire of Testimony

The Spirit Himself is the **Witness of all witnesses**.
When believers pray in the Spirit, they are not sending petitions upward; they are standing *within* the Fire where verdicts are issued.

Heaven's court has no bureaucracy; it operates in pure Spirit.

- **The Spirit of Wisdom** opens the scrolls of remembrance.

- **The Spirit of Understanding** interprets the evidence.

- **The Spirit of Counsel** drafts the decrees.

- **The Spirit of Might** enforces the rulings.

- **The Spirit of Knowledge** records the outcomes.

- **The Spirit of the Fear of the Lord** sanctifies the witnesses.

- **The Spirit of Judgment and Burning** executes purification and seals the verdicts.

Each function flows as a courtroom circuit where the Ekklesia acts as both *jury and instrument* of divine will.

Soulogy — The Renewed Mind as Bench of Reason

When the mind is renewed, it becomes a *bench of divine thought*.
Reason sanctified by the Word transforms into judgment.
In the Courtroom of Heaven, the renewed soul does not argue opinion; it **interprets evidence in the mind of Christ**.

"Come now, and let us reason together, saith the

149

LORD..." — Isaiah 1:18

Intercession begins as a burden, but matures into understanding.

The mature intercessor carries the reasoning of God, knowing why a nation is weighed, why a season shifts, and why mercy must be extended or judgment released.

The Ekklesia, therefore, is not a chorus of pleas; it is a **council of divine logic** seated in mercy and truth.

Physiology — The Body as Legal Instrument

Every part of the body becomes part of the courtroom's function:

Member	Spiritual Function	Courtroom Role
Heart	Altar of worship	Seat of Mercy
Mind	Seat of understanding	Judicial Bench
Hands	Acts of obedience	Execution of decrees
Feet	Evangelistic authority	Enforcement across territories
Tongue	Prophetic instrument	Mouthpiece of law

Eyes	Spiritual perception	Witness recorders
Blood	The covenantal flow	Seal of verdicts

When the body aligns with the Spirit, it becomes the *temple-court-throne triad*:

Worship establishes atmosphere, intercession activates jurisdiction, and decree manifests government.

Theology — The Structure of the Court

The Courtroom of Heaven is not metaphor; it is divine reality. Scripture shows its hierarchy:

1. **The Father** — Supreme Judge (*Psalm 75:7*)

2. **The Son** — Advocate and King (*1 John 2:1*)

3. **The Spirit** — Executor and Witness (*Romans 8:16*)

4. **The Saints** — Co-judges and administrators (*1 Corinthians 6:2*)

5. **Angels** — Recorders and messengers of verdicts (*Daniel 7:10*)

6. **The Blood** — Ever-speaking evidence (*Hebrews 12:24*)

7. **The Word** — Eternal constitution (*Psalm 119:89*)

Every ruling from Heaven flows through this hierarchy, and the Ekklesia participates not as defendants but as **partners of the Judge**.

When Jesus said, *"Whatever you bind on earth shall be bound in heaven"* (*Matthew 16:19*), He was initiating the Church into *judicial cooperation.*

Chronology — From Tabernacle to Throne

The evolution of worship has always been the evolution of government.

1. **In the Wilderness** — the tabernacle was judgment in shadow.

2. **In Zion** — the temple became judgment in song.

3. **At Pentecost** — the believers became judgment in body.

4. **In the End-Time Church** — the Ekklesia becomes judgment in dominion.

Each era moves the worshipper closer to the courtroom, from offering sacrifices *for* the people to executing verdicts *with* God. The prophetic Church of this hour is not waiting for judgment; she **is the embodiment of divine justice** in the earth.

Typology — David's Tabernacle and Heaven's Protocol

David's tent was a prototype of the courtroom-worship dynamic.
Unlike Moses' order, where priests stood outside, David placed singers directly before the ark; worship as legal protocol.
Each psalm was a legal pronouncement, each instrument a covenantal sound.

> *"Let the high praises of God be in their mouth, and a two-edged sword in their hand." — Psalm 149:6*

This union of praise and sword is the true identity of the Ekklesia: **legislative worship**.
When the Bride sings, Heaven rules; when she decrees, nations

tremble.

Technology — The Mechanics of Spiritual Legislation

Heaven's government operates by unbreakable spiritual laws:

1. **Alignment Protocol** — Worship aligns the atmosphere; without alignment, decrees are powerless.

2. **Scroll Protocol** — Every decree must match a written scroll (*Revelation 5:1–10*).

3. **Blood Protocol** — All verdicts are sealed by the Blood of the Lamb.

4. **Voice Protocol** — Only those whose voice harmonises with Christ's intercession carry authority (*John 10:27*).

5. **Fire Protocol** — The Spirit of Judgment and Burning confirms every verdict with purifying flame.

These technologies make the Ekklesia the *most advanced governmental system* in all creation; not digital, but spiritual, not mechanical, but living.

Worship as Judgment

True worship carries verdicts.
When the Spirit fills the temple, as in *2 Chronicles 5*, judgment begins; not condemnation, but divine alignment.
Worship judges disorder by establishing order; it removes idols by enthroning presence.
Every hallelujah spoken in Spirit is a **legal declaration of sovereignty**.

Worship is not escape; it is enforcement.
It does not flee from the world's chaos; it legislates over it until creation bows.

Intercession as Lawmaking

Intercession begins as a plea but matures into policy.
A mature intercessor does not beg for what is already decreed; they **enforce written law**.
When the Church prays in oneness, it is not lobbying Heaven; it is activating existing verdicts.
Every nation has scrolls written in Heaven, and the Ekklesia's intercession unseals them through repentance, decree, and agreement.

In this way, prayer becomes governance, and tears become ink for divine legislation.

The Assembly of Thrones in Session

The corporate Ekklesia, when gathered in the Spirit of unity, is not a congregation but a **heavenly senate**.
Each heart burns as a menorah; each voice releases light into the court.
When the assembly rises in agreement, the court moves into judgment.
Heaven's silence ends, and the roar of Zion begins.

> *"Until the thrones were set, and the Ancient of Days did sit..." — Daniel 7:9*

That moment has come again; the thrones are being set on earth, within believers who have become the living ark of the covenant.
Through them, Heaven legislates.

Prophetic Declaration — The Church in Session

O sons and daughters of Zion, enter the courtroom with fire.

You are not spectators of judgment; you are thrones of enforcement.

Your worship carries verdicts; your intercession writes law.

Let your words be weighed in the scales of mercy and truth; let your hearts burn with the Spirit of judgment and burning.

Speak, decree, and establish; for the Lamb has opened the seals, and the Ekklesia has taken her seat.

Now is the hour when the Courtroom of Heaven and the Assembly of Thrones become one reality; the Church ascended, legislating, and reigning from Zion.

"Out of Zion, the perfection of beauty, God hath shined."
— Psalm 50:2

CHAPTER 22

*The Keys of the Kingdom:
Legislative Power of the Saints*

"And I will give unto thee the keys of the kingdom of heaven: and whatsoever thou shalt bind on earth shall be bound in heaven: and whatsoever thou shalt loose on earth shall be loosed in heaven." — Matthew 16:19 (KJV)

I. Spiritology — The Breath of Dominion

*T*he keys of the Kingdom are not metal instruments but spiritual breath codes; vibrations of divine authority that proceed from the Spirit of Judgment and Burning dwelling in the believer. When Jesus said, "Receive ye the Holy Ghost," He was imparting legislative breath, enabling man to speak as heaven speaks.

- **Keys** represent *entrance and execution;* the power to open spiritual gates, unlock mysteries, and seal verdicts.

- **Binding and loosing** are not rituals but *judicial decrees* that synchronise earth with heaven's will.

- The Spirit of Judgment (to bind) and the Spirit of Burning (to loose) operate together, purging what defiles and establishing what is pure.
When the saints legislate through the Spirit, they breathe divine law into creation.

II. Soulogy — The Alignment of Will and Word

Within the soul, keys operate as *conviction and consent*. The renewed mind must agree with heaven's pattern before authority manifests.

- The *mind* discerns the will of God; the *heart* believes the decree; the *mouth* executes it.

- A divided soul cannot legislate; binding without purity leads to witchcraft, and loosing without discernment leads to rebellion.
Thus, the Church's soul must be harmonised with the Spirit's judgments. When the inner court (conscience) agrees with the heavenly court, decrees carry power that cannot be resisted.
The mature ekklesia learns to bind every thought contrary to Christ and loose the flow of divine peace over nations, regions, and families.

III. Physiology — The Body as Instrument of Legislation

The physical body of the believer becomes a *gate of enforcement*. Hands, feet, and voice function as *instruments of dominion* through which spiritual verdicts are enacted.

- The **mouth** releases decrees; the **hands** perform signs; the **feet** tread upon territorial altars.

- The **blood of Jesus** within our covenant redefines human

DNA as *royal priesthood circuitry* capable of hosting divine rulership.

- Every binding or loosing act becomes visible when the body aligns with the Spirit; fasting, posture, anointing, and even physical presence can shift atmospheres because the throne dwells within the body-temple.

When Christ's body operates in unity, it becomes the physical expression of heaven's government on earth; the embodiment of the legislative Kingdom.

IV. Theology — The Judicial Framework of Heaven

The keys of the Kingdom are judicial instruments derived from Christ's enthronement.

- *To bind* = to restrict, prohibit, and sentence according to the law of righteousness.

- *To loose* = to release, redeem, and restore according to mercy and truth.
  Each decree functions within heaven's *Constitution;* the Word sealed by the Blood and witnessed by the Spirit.
  Christ's death disarmed principalities; His resurrection reestablished dominion; His ascension distributed *keys* to His Body. Thus, every saint who stands in His name functions as part of heaven's Supreme Court.

In this court, the **Throne of the Lamb** is both Judge and Advocate; verdict and mercy united. The Church does not pray to change heaven's mind; it legislates to manifest heaven's will.

V. Chronology — The Prophetic Timeline of Authority

The keys were not given to man in Eden but restored in Christ.

- **Adam** lost legislative power through disobedience.

- **Moses** held shadow keys through the Law.

- **David** sang governmental decrees through worship.

- **Christ** fulfilled all patterns, received the master key of death and Hades, and handed the royal set to His Bride.

Now, in the **seventh-day dispensation**, the ekklesia functions as the Sabbath government; resting while reigning. Every decree issued from this rest carries the weight of eternity because it proceeds from finished works.

VI. Typology — Keys, Thrones, and Gates

Throughout Scripture, keys signify delegated dominion:

- **Key of David** (*Isaiah 22:22*): access to divine governance through worship and intimacy.

- **Keys of Death and Hades** (*Revelation 1:18*): triumph over legal captivity.

- **Keys of the Kingdom** (*Matthew 16:19*): authority to establish heaven's constitution on earth.
  Each key represents a dimension of Christ's rule, and the Church holds the full ring: prophetic authority in worship, judicial authority in prayer, and legislative authority in decree.
  Thus, the binding and loosing are not random acts but the execution of covenant law through covenant intimacy.

VII. Technology — The Operation of Heavenly Systems

The technology of the keys operates through divine order:

1. **Revelation** — Heaven discloses intent.

2. **Interpretation** — The Spirit of Understanding aligns human reason with divine law.

3. **Decree** — The Word is spoken from the position of rest.

4. **Execution** — Angels and spiritual forces carry out the law.

5. **Record** — Every verdict is archived in the Lamb's Book of Life or the books of nations.

Heaven functions as a government of code and sound; the saints, through the Spirit, become administrators of that code: binding the counterfeit frequencies of darkness and loosing the symphonies of divine truth.

The Manifesto of Dominion

To hold the keys is to share in Christ's government. To use them is to enforce His reign.
When the Body of Christ legislates in unity, hell trembles; not because of volume but because of verdict. The gates of hell cannot prevail against the gates of Zion, for Zion's gates are built from eternal decree.

> *"Open ye the gates, that the righteous nation which keepeth the truth may enter in." — Isaiah 26:2*

The final government of heaven is not merely spiritual; it is legislative, judicial, and incarnational. The saints are not beggars before God; they are sons upon the throne, legislators of eternal order.

CHAPTER 23

The Pillars and Gates of Zion: The Architecture of Divine Access

"For he looked for a city which hath foundations, whose builder and maker is God." — Hebrews 11:10 (KJV)
"Her gates shall praise the LORD; her foundations are in the holy mountains." — Psalm 87:1–2

I. Spiritology — The Living Structure of the Spirit

Zion is not built of stone but of spirits made perfect (Hebrews 12:22–23). Its architecture is living fire; each pillar a spirit filled with divine intelligence, each gate a passage of spiritual frequency.

- **Pillars** represent *stability and witness* — the spiritual forces that uphold divine order.

- **Gates** represent *access and legislation* — portals through which decrees flow and nations enter into light.
  In the Spirit, Zion's city is a breathing organism — every saint a stone, every overcomer a pillar, every gate a spiritual

authority of entry.

The **Spirit of Judgment and Burning** dwells within these structures, refining what enters and purifying what proceeds. No unclean thing passes through her gates because her foundations are consecrated fire.

Each gate sings a note; together, the twelve gates create the harmony of the Lamb's government: the sound of divine access restored to creation.

II. Soulogy — The Inner Architecture of Access

The soul itself mirrors Zion's structure.

- The **mind** is a *gate of thought.*

- The **heart** is a *gate of emotion and affection.*

- The **will** is a *gate of decision and dominion.*

When the soul aligns with the Spirit, these gates open upward toward God; when defiled, they open downward toward bondage. Thus, the restoration of the soul is the rebuilding of Zion's gates within man.

The **pillars of the soul** are virtues: truth, purity, humility, faith, love, endurance, and reverence. When these pillars stand, the gates of glory lift up.

> *"Lift up your heads, O ye gates; and be ye lift up, ye everlasting doors; and the King of glory shall come in."*
> *— Psalm 24:7*

The soul becomes a sanctuary when its gates welcome only the King of Glory and reject the traffic of darkness.

III. Physiology — The Body as the Temple of Access

The body is Zion's visible architecture on earth.

- The **eyes** are gates of vision.

- The **ears** are gates of hearing.

- The **mouth** is a gate of decree.

- The **hands and feet** are pillars of movement and dominion.

When the Holy Spirit sanctifies the body, these gates become instruments of divine access; heaven enters earth through human obedience.

The righteous body becomes a *living temple*, where divine currents flow freely between the heavenly court and earthly manifestation.

Every gesture, step, and utterance can open or close a spiritual gate; every act of holiness builds another layer in Zion's wall.

Thus, our physical lives become architecture; shaped by obedience, sealed by blood, and illuminated by glory.

IV. Theology — The Blueprint of Holy Government

Zion's architecture reflects heaven's government.

- The **pillars** correspond to the seven Spirits of God — they uphold the Throne's weight.

- The **gates** correspond to the twelve tribes — they express divine inheritance and order.

- The **foundations** correspond to the twelve apostles — the doctrinal alignment of eternal truth.

Together, they form the eternal constitution of God's dwelling:

Foundation — Apostolic truth.

Pillars — Spiritual forces of righteousness.

Gates — Access points of covenant inheritance.

Glory — The King enthroned in the midst.

Thus, Zion is not a mystical ideal but the *operational centre of divine governance*. When the ekklesia walks in unity and purity, the pattern of Zion manifests in the earth; the invisible city becomes visible through holy community.

V. Chronology — From Eden to New Jerusalem

The story of divine access begins in **Eden**, where man lost the gate of communion. Two cherubim with flaming swords guarded the entrance, sealing the way until redemption.

At **Sinai**, God reintroduced structure: pillars of testimony and gates of covenant.

In **David's Zion**, the ark returned, symbolising restored access through worship.

Through **Christ**, the veil was torn: the central gate reopened.

In the **New Jerusalem**, the full architecture is complete: twelve gates of pearl, each speaking of suffering turned to glory; twelve foundations of precious stones, each reflecting divine nature perfected in man.

Thus, the entire biblical timeline is an architectural project; heaven rebuilding its dwelling within man and through man.

VI. Typology — The Symbolic Order of Pillars and Gates

Throughout Scripture:

- **Pillars** signify *witness, covenant, and establishment.*

  - *Jacob* raised a pillar at Bethel (**Genesis 28:18**) — revelation pillar.

  - *Moses* set twelve pillars for the tribes (**Exodus 24:4**) — covenant pillar.

- *Samson* pulled down the pillars of Dagon's house (*Judges 16:29*) — overthrow of false government.

- *Paul* called James, Cephas, and John "pillars" (*Galatians 2:9*) — apostolic foundation.

- **Gates** signify *transition, access, and governance.*

  - *Lot sat at the gate* (*Genesis 19:1*) — judicial seat of decision.

  - *The elders sat in the gates* (*Ruth 4:1*) — legal transactions.

  - *Nehemiah rebuilt the gates of Jerusalem* — restoration of order.

  - *The twelve gates of* **Revelation 21** — eternal accessibility of the redeemed.

Each pillar and gate embodies a spiritual technology; when restored, they become the infrastructure through which heaven flows into earth.

VII. Technology — The Operations of Access

Heaven's architecture functions through spiritual technologies:

1. **Gate Protocols** — Worship opens, disobedience shuts. Every gate operates by the law of holiness.

2. **Pillar Protocols** — Alignment and balance. Every pillar bears the name of a Spirit: Wisdom, Understanding, Counsel, Might, Knowledge, Judgment, Burning.

3. **Foundation Protocols** — Truth systems anchored in the apostolic Word.

4. **Gatekeepers and Porters** — Angels, elders, and priests who monitor spiritual entry points.

5. **Sound Technology** — Trumpets, psalms, and decrees open

gates of light or shut gates of darkness.

When the ekklesia learns to synchronise these protocols, heaven and earth merge into one seamless domain: Zion manifesting through human cooperation.

The Manifesto of Access

Zion is not a mountain far away; it is the divine architecture of man restored. Every saint is a living pillar, every righteous decree a gate of glory.

When the Church stands as the architecture of divine access, nothing in creation remains closed; every gate lifts its head, every nation encounters light.

> *"I will make him a pillar in the temple of my God, and he shall go no more out."* — *Revelation 3:12*
> *"And the nations of them which are saved shall walk in the light of it."* — *Revelation 21:24*

Through the Spirit of Judgment and Burning, the foundations are purified; through the Lamb, the gates are opened; through the Bride, the city descends.

This is the architecture of divine access: Zion built in man, God dwelling in His temple, heaven established upon earth.

CHAPTER 24

*The Seven Thrones of Light: How the
Spirit Rules Through the Ekklesia*

(*The Crown Circuit of Dominion*)

> "And out of the throne proceeded lightnings and
> thunderings and voices: and there were seven lamps
> of fire burning before the throne, which are the seven
> Spirits of God." — **Revelation 4:5**
> "Thy throne, O God, is for ever and ever: the sceptre of
> thy kingdom is a right sceptre." — **Psalm 45:6**

I. Spiritology — The Thrones of Fire Within the Throne

*E*very government requires a council of light; heaven's own
government flows through seven thrones of light, each one a
living flame: the Spirit of Wisdom, Understanding, Counsel,
Might, Knowledge, Judgment, and Burning.

These are not mere attributes; they are beings of administration, divine intelligences through which the Holy Spirit executes the Father's will in creation.

Each throne burns as a circuit of government within the Ekklesia:

- **Wisdom** governs **purpose** — knowing what Heaven intends.

- **Understanding** governs **structure** — how Heaven builds.

- **Counsel** governs **strategy** — how Heaven advances.

- **Might** governs **execution** — how Heaven enforces.

- **Knowledge** governs **accuracy** — how Heaven interprets.

- **Judgment** governs **alignment** — how Heaven separates.

- **Burning** governs **purity** — how Heaven sustains holy fire.

Together, they form one throne; the **Spirit of the Lord enthroned in sevenfold administration**.
Thus, the Ekklesia is not a gathering of opinions but a **circuit of light;** seven thrones seated within one body, radiating divine rule through every domain of creation.

II. Soulogy — The Seven Thrones in the Inner Kingdom

The soul of the believer is the **chamber of enthronement**.
When the Spirit of God fills the soul, these seven thrones are activated within the inner court of man:

- The **mind** receives Wisdom and Understanding.

- The **heart** receives Counsel and Knowledge.

- The **will** receives Might and Judgment.

- The **conscience** becomes the altar of Burning.

Here, the believer becomes a microcosm of Zion; a living temple where the seven thrones rule inwardly before they manifest outwardly.

Every decision becomes a decree; every thought becomes architecture; every affection becomes law.
The soul thus graduates from *emotion-led living* to *throne-led governance.*

The mature Ekklesia is not led by moods but by **thronal intelligence;** a sanctified consciousness where each Spirit governs a gate of the soul.

III. Physiology — The Body as the Conduit of Thrones

The body is the **instrument of manifestation** for the thrones of light.

- **Eyes** transmit Wisdom and Knowledge.

- **Ears** discern Counsel and Judgment.

- **Hands** enforce Might and Righteousness.

- **Feet** walk in Understanding and Dominion.

Thus, the believer's physical life becomes the government's extension.
When yielded fully, the human vessel becomes a conduit of divine operation; healing, decree, and deliverance flow as thronal acts through embodied obedience.

This is why the resurrected Christ *still bears a body;* for government requires form.
The Ekklesia, as the Body of Christ, is the visible throne-room of the invisible Spirit.

> *"Thy kingdom come, thy will be done, in earth, as it is in heaven."*

Every motion of the Body is meant to express the movement of Heaven's light.

IV. Theology — The Doctrine of Sevenfold Dominion

The doctrine of the seven thrones reveals the full governmental theology of the Spirit.

Each throne is both **a domain of revelation** and **a mantle of rule**:

Spirit	Function	Domain of Government
Wisdom	Establishes divine purpose	Creation & design
Understanding	Builds the structure of truth	Doctrine & revelation
Counsel	Directs divine strategy	Leadership & intercession
Might	Executes power and conquest	Warfare & miracles
Knowledge	Interprets divine order	Prophecy & discernment
Judgment	Separates light from darkness	Justice & alignment
Burning	Purifies and sustains	Worship & consecration

The Church must return to this **sevenfold theology,** not denominational fragments but divine wholeness.

These thrones are not optional gifts; they are the **governing infrastructure of the Kingdom.**

To reject one Spirit is to lose one pillar of dominion. To honour all is to reign as Zion.

V. Chronology — From Lucifer's Fall to the Lamb's Reign

Chronologically, the seven thrones trace the history of divine administration:

1. **Before the Fall:** The seven thrones were the original order of heavenly governance.

2. **Lucifer's Rebellion:** He sought to ascend above the stars, attempting to claim dominion over these thrones. His fall left a governmental vacuum that man was created to fill.

3. **Through the Patriarchs:** Each patriarch restored one throne —

   - Noah — Judgment,

   - Abraham — Faith and Counsel,

   - Moses — Law and Understanding,

   - David — Worship and Burning.

4. **Through Christ:** All seven thrones were embodied and enthroned in the Man of Glory.

5. **Through the Church:** The Spirit now distributes the sevenfold reign through the Ekklesia until every throne on earth mirrors those in Heaven.

The story of history is the **reinstallation of thrones;** from rebellion to restoration, from corruption to coronation.

VI. Typology — Thrones, Lamps, and Crowns

Typologically, Scripture is filled with shadows of these seven thrones:

- **Seven Lamps of Fire** (*Revelation 4:5*) — illumination of government.

- **Seven Eyes of the Lamb** (*Revelation 5:6*) — total discernment of divine intelligence.

- **Seven Horns** — complete power and authority.

- **Seven Candlesticks** — the corporate witness of the sevenfold Spirit through the Church.

- **Seven Crowns** — reward of those who reign with Christ.

Every type points to this truth: the **Ekklesia is the composite throne of the sevenfold Spirit.**

Just as the ark of the covenant had the mercy seat overshadowed by two cherubim, so now the Ekklesia carries the entire throne system within her, crowned by the Head, Christ Himself.

VII. Technology — The Operation of the Seven Thrones

Heaven's technology operates through **thronal synchronisation;** when the seven Spirits function in unity through the body of Christ.

This technology is activated by three key operations:

1. **Vision:** Seeing what Heaven decrees — the spirit of Wisdom and Understanding.

2. **Utterance:** Declaring what Heaven speaks — the spirit of Counsel and Might.

3. **Execution:** Performing what Heaven wills — the spirit of Knowledge, Judgment, and Burning.

When these seven lights synchronise, **Zion legislates**.
The Church becomes a live governmental system; not just praying *for* things to happen but *releasing* them as heavenly verdicts.

Every decree becomes light, every prayer a thronal echo, every saint a channel of administration.
Thus, "out of Zion, the perfection of beauty, God hath shined" (*Psalm 50:2*).

The Manifesto of the Seven Thrones

The Ekklesia is the **assembly of thrones**, not an audience of believers.
We were not saved to escape the world but to **govern it through light**.
Each saint is a lamp, each lamp a throne, each throne a ray of the King's dominion.

When these seven thrones operate in unity, the full weight of Christ's government manifests:

- **Wisdom** defines,

- **Understanding** builds,

- **Counsel** directs,

- **Might** enforces,

- **Knowledge** refines,

- **Judgment** aligns,

- **Burning** sustains.

> *"And the government shall be upon His shoulder."*
> — *Isaiah 9:6*

The shoulder is the Church; the light is the Spirit; the throne is the Lamb.

From Zion's summit, the seven thrones now burn in perfect symmetry, governing heaven and earth through the **Ekklesia — the Undisputed Heavyweight Government of God.**

CHAPTER 25

The Fire-Dwelling Kingdom: When Glory Becomes Government

(*The Eternal Seal of Zion's Reign*)

> *"For upon all the glory shall be a defence. And the LORD will create upon every dwelling place of mount Zion... a cloud and smoke by day, and the shining of a flaming fire by night: for upon all the glory shall be a defence."* — Isaiah 4:5
>
> *"Our God is a consuming fire."* — Hebrews 12:29

I. Spiritology — The Final Descent of Fire

When the Spirit of Judgment and Burning fully descends, heaven no longer visits earth; heaven dwells here.

This is not punitive fire but ordering fire; the same presence that once purified the altar now establishes the throne.
It refines until only what is eternal remains.
The Ekklesia becomes the habitation of flame; every saint a coal, every gathering a furnace of divine order.

This fire doesn't destroy the Church; it defines her.

Where the Spirit first hovered over chaos, He now rests upon covenant.

The end of the age is not the ruin of creation but its refinement; when the **Kingdom itself glows with the very glory that judges and renews.**

II. Soulogy — When the Inner Court Becomes Radiant

The Spirit of Burning begins within.

The mind is cleansed of false patterns; the heart is purged of divided affections.

The soul no longer hosts conflict but communion; a still flame where thought, desire, and will move as one.

This inner convergence is how the overcomer rises: when the soul no longer negotiates with darkness, it radiates light.

The true overcomer isn't the loudest intercessor, but the one whose conscience has become transparent enough for glory to flow through unbroken.

III. Physiology — The Body of Fire

The body becomes the visible lampstand of that inward reign.

Hands heal not by effort but by order; words create not by volume but by alignment.

The resurrected Christ revealed a body that could pass through walls yet bear scars;

proof that **glory perfects form without erasing history**.

In the same pattern, the corporate body of Christ will stand as the Fire-Body of the Kingdom: an immortal structure hosting an immortal Spirit.

The very dust of the earth will shimmer with divine law.

IV. Theology — Glory as the Highest Form of Government

Government and glory are not opposites; glory is government fulfilled.
When rule is perfectly righteous, it shines.
This is why the New Jerusalem has no temple: *the Lord God Almighty and the Lamb are the temple thereof.* Law and light have become one.

The Spirit of Judgment and Burning is therefore the **eternal constitution of glory:** He ensures that every manifestation of power remains pure, that the brilliance of dominion never collapses into pride.
He is the Governor of radiance, the balance of holiness and majesty.

V. Chronology — From Pentecost to Parousia

- **At Pentecost,** fire sat upon each head — government began in personal measure.

- **Through the ages,** the flame multiplied — from martyrdom to revival, from hidden monasteries to open movements.

- **In the end,** the fire ceases to visit and begins to *inhabit*: the Bride becomes the flame itself.

What began as tongues of fire concludes as a **city of fire.**
The Ekklesia, once a scattered remnant, ascends as the luminous city; the very infrastructure of the Lamb's eternal rule.

VI. Typology — From Tabernacle to Throne

- **Moses' bush** burned but was not consumed — the type of a nation aflame yet alive.

- **The Temple fire** never went out — a symbol of perpetual presence.

- **The tongues of *Acts 2*** ignited the new priesthood.

- **Revelation's crystal sea mixed with fire** reveals the final assembly — judgment and mercy fused in eternal balance.

Every flame in Scripture has been one long prophecy: the Lord was always building a **Fire-Dwelling Kingdom**, not a flame-visited world.

VII. Technology — How Glory Administers Creation

Heaven's technology in the last age is **radiant governance**.
Decrees are no longer shouted but *emanated*; the saints legislate by presence, not performance.
The Spirit of Burning synchronises the seven thrones into one living frequency; light becomes law, and law becomes life.

This is the technology of transfiguration: where government ceases to be written and begins to shine.
The overcomers become *light-bearers*, transmitting divine order simply by being fully aligned.

The Manifesto of the Fire-Dwelling Kingdom

When the Spirit of Judgment and Burning rests, the following marks appear:

1. **Purity replaces politics** — leadership becomes priesthood.

2. **Light replaces argument** — truth needs no defence when it shines.

3. **Glory replaces ambition** — rule becomes service clothed in majesty.

4. **Ekklesia replaces empire** — one body, many flames.

5. **Sabbath replaces striving** — rest becomes the rhythm of reign.

This is the final metamorphosis: the Ekklesia transfigured into Zion, Zion transfigured into light, and light enthroned as eternal government.

"Upon all the glory shall be a defence."

Glory is the defence because it is also the government.

The Spirit of Judgment and Burning, last of the seven, yet foundation of them all, is the eternal seal of divine order. He ensures that glory will never again be stolen, that thrones will never again fall.

When the Lamb reigns through a body of fire, creation will no longer resist the will of God: it will *reflect* it.

This is the destiny of the Ekklesia:
to become the undisputed, radiant government of the ages; the **Fire-Dwelling Kingdom**, where **Glory has become Government**, and **God rests forever in His light.**

CHAPTER 26

The Glory of the Government: When Heaven and Earth Become One

*I*n this closing revelation, the scroll of the True Church unfolds *its final seal: the union of realms, where divine order and visible creation merge under the reign of the Lamb. This is the completion of the mystery Paul saw and John beheld: "That in the dispensation of the fullness of times He might gather together in one all things in Christ, both which are in heaven, and which are on earth" (Ephesians 1:10). Heaven is not a distant place; it is a dimension of government. Earth is its mirror, awaiting alignment.*

1. The Descent of Glory — Heaven Invading the Earth

When the government of heaven descends, it does not come as a cloud to carry away, but as **a Presence to dwell**. The New Jerusalem is not a city of escape, but a city of embodiment; the Ekklesia fully transformed into the architecture of God's light. The throne no longer dwells in the heavens only, for *"the tabernacle of God is with men"* (**Revelation 21:3**).

The Spirit of Judgment and Burning has refined all vessels; the gold of divine nature shines through redeemed humanity.

Heaven's streets are no longer above, but **within;** every redeemed heart paved with the clarity of transparent gold, minds aligned as gates of pearl, and wills as foundations of precious stones.

2. The Government of Glory — Light as Law

In this realm, the **Spirit of Glory and of God** becomes the constitution. The Lamb is the lamp, and the nations walk in that light.

Government is no longer enforced; it **emanates**. Dominion flows not by decree but by radiance. Every son of Zion becomes a living flame of governance; a priest-king whose worship *is* law, whose adoration *is* judgment.

No temple is needed, for the Lamb and His Bride are the temple. This is not religion; it is divine civilisation, where holiness has become atmosphere, and righteousness, the rhythm of reality.

3. The Harmony of Realms — The Cosmic Sabbath

The seventh day now stretches into eternity. The Sabbath rest becomes the cosmic synchronisation of all creation under the Spirit's rhythm.

The Spirit of Judgment and Burning has removed all mixture; only **pure frequencies of truth** remain.

Heaven and earth sing one song: *"The kingdoms of this world are become the kingdoms of our Lord, and of His Christ"* (**Revelation 11:15**).

Time itself bows — Chronos yields to Kairos, and eternity begins to breathe through every redeemed vessel.

4. The Bride as the Radiant Law of Zion

The Bride now stands unveiled as the living embodiment of divine government: crowned, enthroned, and luminous.

She is no longer just the Church; she is **the City, the Kingdom, and the Glory.**

Every redeemed soul becomes a syllable of the eternal Name; together they form the Word made visible again.

Where once there was intercession, now there is **legislation through love**. Where once there were tears of warfare, now there is laughter of reign.

This is the Ekklesia perfected; **the Lamb's consort in dominion, the Spirit's tabernacle in fire**, and **the Father's delight in completion**.

5. The Eternal Seal — The Spirit of Judgment and Burning

As the book closes, the same Spirit that began the purification now seals the manifestation.

The **Spirit of Judgment and Burning** is not destruction; it is the final sanctification of the cosmos[the fire that turns the creation itself into worship.

This is the **Covenant of Fire** Isaiah foresaw (*Isaiah 4:4*), the cleansing of Zion until her filth is washed away and her assemblies become glory.

The Lamb reigns not only from heaven but **through His Body on earth**. The light of the Throne fills all things.

6. The Final Vision — The Reign of the Lamb

Heaven and earth are one courtroom, one temple, one throne.

The overcomers reign as the reflection of the Lamb's authority — kings without rival, priests without end.

This is the true weight of the Body of Christ: **the undefeated, undivided, unstoppable government of God**.

The scroll ends where eternity begins — with the words written in fire:

> *"And the glory of the LORD shall cover the earth, as the waters cover the sea."*
> *— Habakkuk 2:14*

CHAPTER 27

The Sound Becomes Government:
The Day of the Lord and
the Assembly of Fire

W hen heaven's sound becomes earth's structure, the unseen *Word becomes visible government. Every trumpet, every decree, every tongue of fire spoken from Zion begins to solidify into divine architecture. This is the Day of the Lord, not merely an event of judgment, but the hour when the voice of the Spirit crystallises into law, when worship matures into rulership, and when the sons of God become the living thunder of His dominion.*

1. The Day of the Lord — The Sound of Transition

The Day of the Lord is the transition between two orders: the fading governance of flesh and the rising dominion of Spirit.
It is the day when the **Spirit of Judgment and Burning** speaks through the overcomers, consuming every false system with the brightness of His appearing.
The day dawns not as a date on the calendar but as a **dimension of manifestation;** the unveiling of the Christ nature in a company of perfected saints.
As Malachi prophesied, *"Unto you that fear My name shall the Sun*

of Righteousness arise with healing in His wings" (**Malachi 4:2**).
This day is a sunrise; fire turning into governance, light maturing into law.

2. The Trumpet Becomes a Throne

Every prophetic voice was a rehearsal for this moment. The trumpet was not just a sound; it was **a blueprint vibrating in time**, waiting for bodies through which to rule.
Now, the sound that once shook Sinai rests upon Zion's assembly.
The same voice that thundered through prophets now speaks **through the collective Body**, the Ekklesia filled with the Spirit of Burning.
When this trumpet sounds, it does not call to battle but **calls to enthronement**.
The Church no longer prays for heaven to intervene; heaven prays through her, decrees through her, reigns through her.
The sound has become government.

3. The Assembly of Fire — The Corporate Throne

This is the moment Isaiah foresaw when he said, *"The LORD will create upon every dwelling place of Mount Zion, and upon her assemblies, a cloud and smoke by day, and the shining of a flaming fire by night"* (**Isaiah 4:5**).
Each assembly becomes a **pillar of fire**, and together they form **the Body of the Throne**.
Every saint becomes a living flame within the corporate lampstand of the Lamb.
This is the **Council of Fire**, the Ekklesia joined in eternal agreement; judgment and mercy, light and love fused as one.
Worship no longer ascends; it radiates.
The house of prayer becomes the **house of governance**.

4. The Word That Speaks as Fire

In this age, words no longer carry opinion but nature. Every decree spoken from Zion bears the **essence of the One who sent it**.

As Jeremiah wrote, *"Is not My word like as a fire? saith the LORD; and like a hammer that breaketh the rock in pieces?"* (**Jeremiah 23:29**).

The Spirit of Judgment and Burning has purified the tongue; the altar of speech — until prophecy and law are one voice.

In this realm, intercession is fire, decree is thunder, and revelation is manifestation.

The Church no longer reacts; she **creates**.

Her voice is the continuation of God's own Word; the **ongoing Genesis** of the Kingdom.

5. The Fire That Governs

The fire that once descended now dwells.

The cloud that once guided Israel now fills the inner sanctuary of every redeemed vessel.

This is not revival — it is **habitation**.

The Spirit of Burning is the final form of divine governance; a people who have become fire without being consumed.

Their minds are crystal, their hearts flame, their spirits throne.

They are the reflection of the Lamb who reigns through light.

As Daniel foresaw, *"A fiery stream issued and came forth from before Him: thousand thousands ministered unto Him"* (**Daniel 7:10**).

That stream now flows through the Ekklesia — the river of government proceeding from the throne of the Lamb.

6. The Day of the Assembly — Heaven's Final Manifestation

The Day of the Lord culminates in the **Assembly of Fire;** heaven and earth united in one symphony of light.

Every nation stands before this radiance, not to be condemned but to be transformed by truth.

Judgment has become purification. Dominion has become worship.

The sound that once warned now welcomes — *"Come, ye blessed of My Father, inherit the kingdom prepared for you."*

This is the **Eternal Sabbath**, the **government of peace**, the **Kingdom of Fire and Light**.

7. The Final Witness — Glory Translated into Dominion

The scroll closes where eternity opens: the sound that began in Genesis — *"Let there be light"* now echoes through redeemed creation as, *"Let there be glory."*

Every throned son becomes a note in that song. Every burning spirit becomes a facet of His face.

The sound that once spoke from heaven now rules **through His Body**, and that Body is **the government of God in the earth**.

And the Spirit of Judgment and Burning seals the book with one decree:

> *"For the LORD shall arise upon thee, and His glory shall be seen upon thee. And the nations shall come to thy light, and kings to the brightness of thy rising."*
> *— Isaiah 60:2–3*

PART VII

THE FINAL DOMINION SCROLL

CHAPTER 28

*Thrones, Keys, and the River of
Government — The Architecture
of Spiritual Jurisdiction*

*T*he true Church was never born to resemble an audience.
She was designed as a **Courtroom, a Council, a City, and a
Government:**
Heaven's executive branch embodied in redeemed humanity.

Religion filled pews; revelation built thrones.
Tradition chased titles; Heaven forged jurisdictions.
For every throne is a **seat of rule**, and every key is a **right
of access**, and together they form the blueprint of divine
government: **a living architecture where the unseen becomes
law.**

1. The Pattern From Heaven — Moses and the Transfer of Jurisdiction

When Moses sat to judge Israel (*Exodus 18:13–16*), he was not
acting as a village elder.
He was rehearsing Heaven's constitution.
The weighty cases rising upward revealed a tiered government; a

throne dimension followed by key administration.

This pattern would later be fulfilled in Christ, the greater Moses, who stood before His disciples and declared:

> *"I give unto you the keys of the kingdom of heaven."* — *Matthew 16:19*

With those words, Heaven transferred jurisdiction.
The throne of David expanded into the Body of Christ.
A new council formed on earth; **the Ekklesia: kings and priests seated in heavenly places, legislating righteousness into the earth.**

2. Thrones — Seats of Light, Judgment, and Dominion

A throne is not furniture; it is frequency.
It is the stabilised atmosphere of divine order.

Every believer carries a throne within because Christ reigns in the heart.
Where that inner throne is honoured, a domain forms around it:

• Family
• Territory
• Calling
• City
• Nation

Psalm 89:14 names the constitution of all governmental thrones:

> *"Righteousness and judgment are the habitation of His throne."*

When the Ekklesia sits in that habitation,

her words become verdicts.
Her decrees are witnessed by fire.
Her rulings shift unseen infrastructures.

3. Keys — Instruments of Access and Administration

Keys do not symbolise authority; they *authorise* it.
In the Spirit, every revelation is a key; a code, a clearance, an access-point.

Without keys: zeal becomes noise.
With keys: dominion becomes effortless.

Isaiah foresaw Christ carrying the master key:

> *"The key of the house of David… he shall open, and none shall shut." — Isaiah 22:22*

Now that key rests upon His Body.
Every saint receives specific keys:
worship, governance, healing, deliverance, wisdom, creation.

When used under the Spirit's witness, gates open.
When used outside jurisdiction, heaven remains silent.

4. The Architecture of Spiritual Jurisdiction

The Ekklesia is not an institution; it is a **living constitution**.

- **Thrones define rule.**
- **Keys administer authority.**
- **Altars sustain fire and witness.**
- **Scrolls record verdicts and decrees.**

Where these four align, Heaven's government becomes visible. Where they are absent, religion imitates power but never enforces it.

In the invisible world, jurisdiction is recognition.
What Heaven recognises, creation yields to.
When a saint decrees within the assigned jurisdiction, the decree becomes law.
Outside it, words fall without witness.

5. Priest-King Integration — The Balance of Governance

The throne governs.
The altar sanctifies.

Kingship without priesthood becomes tyranny.
Priesthood without kingship becomes sentiment.
The true Ekklesia carries both mandate and mercy braided together.
From this balance flows legislation that heals nations.

6. The Courtroom Pattern — Heaven's Operating System

Heaven's legal structure is the template for earthly governance:

• The Father presides as Judge.
• The Son stands as Advocate and King.
• The Spirit executes as Fire and Witness.
• The saints serve as co-judges, echoing verdicts written in light.

When the Church gathers, she is not singing *toward* the throne —

she is seated *with* the throne.

Worship becomes legislation.
Praise becomes procedure.
Every "Amen" seals a verdict.

7. The Seven-Dimensional Revelation

Spiritology:
The throne is the indwelling presence; the key is the breath that

unlocks realms.

Soulogy:
The renewed mind forms a courtroom, discerning permitted vs. forbidden.

Physiology:
The body becomes a gate; hands decree, feet occupy, mouth legislates.

Theology:
Father governs; Son embodies law; Spirit executes.

Chronology:
Adam ruled from a throne; David embodied it; the Lamb eternalised it.

Typology:
Moses' judgeship prefigures Christ's global Ekklesia.
Keys of David become keys of the Kingdom.

Technology:
Revelation is the operating system; decrees are data; altars are servers;
the Spirit is the power grid transmitting governmental flow.

8. The Call to Sit — Entering the Rest of Government

The Spirit is summoning the Church to stop standing before the throne
and start sitting with it.

To sit is to rest; not inactivity, but governmental stabilisation.
From rest comes legislation.
From union comes execution.

Where thrones are established, darkness is displaced.
Where keys turn, destiny unlocks.
The true Church rises not by size but by jurisdiction.

9. The River and the City — Government as Living Circulation

"And he shewed me a pure river of water of life..." —
Revelation 22:1

The throne is not a monument; it is movement.
Government flows. It circulates.
It pulses through creation like a bloodstream.

Ezekiel saw waters issuing from the temple:
waters of repentance, intercession, authority, and glory.

The City (the Bride) is built around this river:
walls of salvation, gates of praise, foundations of apostles,
and ministries as trees of life fed by a continual flow.

Where this river flows, death dissolves.
Where this current moves, rebellion yields.

10. When Government Becomes Life

The highest expression of dominion is circulation:
not control, but transformation.

The Throne is the heart.
The Lamb is the blood.
The Spirit is the flow.
The Ekklesia is the Body.
The River is the life that unites them.

When the Church understands this, she stops protecting
territory and starts governing flow.

11. Signs the Ekklesia Is Becoming Fire-Dwelling

• Words perform.

- Worship becomes protocol.
- Trials refine without breaking authority.
- Nations respond; doors open, false thrones collapse.
- Prayer becomes preemptive decree.

12. Warnings & Legal Ethics of Dominion

Fire expands capacity but exposes flaws.

- **Accountability:** every throne answers upward.
- **Humility:** Authority carries responsibility to the weak.
- **Truth:** prophetic law must align with Scripture and fruit.

Authority without ethics becomes ash.

13. The Final Decree — The Prophetic Charge

*"Arise, bearers of flame.
Let your private sanctuaries remain pure,
your public councils lawful,
your decrees aligned with the Lamb.
From altar to city, from breath to law;
let Glory be known as Government."*

14. Benediction

Reader: "The gavel of the Throne strikes once."
Assembly: "By the Blood, by the Fire, and by the Word; let what was visited now dwell. Amen."

CHAPTER 29

The Keys and Seals of Dominion (Binding, Loosing, and Legislative Power)

Authority is not noise — it is legal execution.

*T*he keys of the Kingdom are not magic; they are **divine protocols,** *means by which Heaven's jurisprudence is enacted through obedient human vessels. The seals are Heaven's signature, the finalisation of a verdict that moves from throne to terrain.*

I. Core Thesis — What Keys, Binding, Loosing, and Seals Actually Are

- **Keys** = delegated authority & operational codes (revelation + stewardship).

- **Binding** = a judicial act that restricts or arrests illegitimate activity or legal rights held by darkness. It is performed against unlawful spiritual claims, not people.

- **Loosing** = a judicial act that restores permission, destiny, deliverance, or release according to Heaven's law.

- **Seals** = the Spirit's ratification; a binding in the invisible realm that makes a decree enduring and enforceable by angelic administration.

These are legal acts performed by those who have learned Heaven's law, not weapons of wilful coercion. They always require alignment with the Word, the Blood, and the Spirit.

II. Seven-Dimensional Map (How keys & seals function across the Word)

Dimension	What it means	How keys/seals function here
Spiritology	Breath & witness of God	Keys are breathed revelation; seals are the Spirit's stamp.
Soulogy	Mind, will, emotion	Binding/loosing begins with inner assent — conscience as courtroom bench.
Physiology	Body as instrument	Voice, posture, fasting, touch — the body enacts decrees.
Theology	Divine constitution	All acts must align with Christ's finished work (Blood + Word).
Chronology	Timing & seasons	Decrees follow kairos (appointed time) — not impatience.

Typology	Biblical patterns	Moses (judicial pattern), David (worship + authority), Elijah (prophetic decree).
Technology	Spiritual mechanics	Sound, decree, scroll metaphor — angels as executors, seals as access tokens.

III. Courtroom Protocol — How to Legislate Lawfully (Practical steps)

1. Ascend — posture & purity

- Begin in worship/quietness. Enter by the Blood. Confess privately and corporately. No legal action without a clean altar.

2. Receive — hear the case from Heaven

- Wait for a clear witness of the Spirit or a Scripture that frames the legal basis. Record it.

3. Gather evidence — Scripture + testimony

- Quote the Word (primary evidence). Produce witness testimony (answered prayer, prophetic confirmation, fruit).

4. Declare — binding or loosing

- Speak the legal language clearly, present tense, short and scriptural. Use "By the authority of Jesus Christ" & reference scripture when possible.

5. Seal — sign & ratify

- Invoke the Blood and the Spirit of Judgment & Burning: "By the Blood of Jesus and the seal of the Holy Spirit, we seal this decree."

6. Execute — dispatch

- Commission angels, pray for visible obedience, act in obedience (practical step), and record testimony. Expect spiritual enforcement.

7. Log & testify

- Keep records — who participated, scriptural basis, timing, and outcomes. This forms the Ekklesia's witness book.

IV. Sample Forms — Legal Language You Can Adapt

Notes: Keep statements short, scriptural, and targeted. Don't maledict individuals. Bind systems, spirits, strongholds; loose destiny, healing, access, and blessing.

A. Binding (example — spiritual stronghold)

"In the name of Jesus Christ, by the authority given to the Body of Christ, we bind the legal rights and assignments of the spirit of _____ over this family/city/area. We bind every legal agreement, covenant, and ungodly transfer. We arrest your operations and revoke your decrees, and we render you powerless by the Blood of Jesus. You are bound — legal ground removed. Amen."

B. Loosing (example — release of destiny)

"By the Blood of Jesus and the authority of the keys entrusted to the Church, we loose the destiny, gifts and harvest prepared for [person/place]. We open the gates of provision, revelation and favour; we release healing and restoration; we declare this path lawful before God. Amen."

C. Sealing (ratification)

"We seal this decree by the Spirit of Judgment and Burning. By the Blood of the Lamb and the seal of the Holy Spirit, this word is established in heaven and sent to the earth. Let angels execute and return testimony. So it stands."

V. The Sealing Liturgy — Corporate Template (short)

1. Worship 2–5 minutes (focus on throne).

2. Reader: "We have presented the case before the Court of Heaven."

3. Leader: Reads scriptural warrant.

4. Assembly: Decree the binding/loosing (short statements).

5. Leader: "By the Blood and by the Spirit, we now seal this verdict."

6. All: "Sealed in Heaven; executed on Earth."

7. Dispatch (song or prayer of sending angels).

VI. Biblical Case Studies — How the Pattern Operates (brief)

- **Abraham pleading (*Genesis 18*)** — Intercessory litigation: he argues for legal mercy on behalf of the righteous. Key principle: covenant memory as a legal basis.

- **Elijah (*1 Kings 17–18*)** — Decree that produced drought and later rain: prophetic verdicts enforced by heaven because they stood on God's covenant and voice.

- **Jesus (*Matthew 16:19 / 18:18*)** — Keys given as judicial authority to bind/loose corporate and local jurisdiction.

- **Revelation (seals & scrolls)** — Only the Lamb opens seals — authority resides in Christ but is executed through His Body after alignment.

VII. Discernment Checklist (Before you bind/loose)

- Is there **Scriptural warrant**? (primary)

- Do you have **inner witness** (Spirit) and **outer confirmation** (prophetic, apostolic, corporate)?

- Has personal or corporate **repentance** taken place for relevant sin?

- Is there **accountability** (someone overseeing, elders, apostolic covering)?

- Will the action **help liberation and restoration** or vent spiritual malice?

- Are there **practical steps** you will take following the decree?

If any answer is "no," pause. Keys without wisdom cause damage.

VIII. Ethics & Safeguards (Non-negotiable)

- **Never** use binding to attack, manipulate, or coerce people's consciences. Target systems, spirits, and legalities, not persons.

- **Always** scripturalise the work. The Word is the court's constitution.

- **Always** include mercy and restoration in your loosing language. Kingdom law aims to restore, not wreck.

- **Maintain accountability.** Elders/covering must ratify major corporate decrees.

- **Log every act.** Keep minutes, scriptures used, witnesses, and outcomes. The Body must be a responsible steward.

IX. Operational Exercises — Training the Court

1. Case Practice (small groups)

- Read one short passage (e.g., *Psalm 89*). Determine a binding/loosing application, find supporting scripture, present it, and receive elder feedback.

2. Sealing Drill (corporate)

- After a 10-minute prophetic report, practice a 60-second sealing liturgy as a group, then record anything that shifts in 72 hours.

3. Accountability Rotation

- Rotate elders who review proposed decrees each month. Training builds maturity.

X. When Things Don't Shift — Troubleshooting

- **No immediate change:** check legal ground; is there unconfessed sin, unrepented covenant, or required action?

- **Backlash or confusion:** stop, confess, reassess. Not every resistance is demonic; some are delays for obedience.

- **False claims of results:** insist on documentation. Kingdom administration values testimony and record.

XI. Prophetic Charge — The Responsible Use of Keys

You have been entrusted with keys. Keys carry weight. They are not for spectacle but stewardship. The Body that learns to bind with justice and to loose with mercy becomes the instrument of God's government. The seals they place become the laws that angels execute.

"Open the doors that are lawful; close the doors that are illicit. Hold fast to mercy; let justice walk in your courts. Sit in the seat of authority with humility and the gavel of fire."

XII. Short Prayers to Use (one each)

For Clarity before a Decree:
"Father, give us Your clear warrant. Let no word be spoken but that which comes from Your throne. Holy Spirit, witness; Lord Jesus, cover us with Your Blood. Amen."

For Binding:
"By the authority of Jesus Christ and according to Your Word, we hereby bind the legal rights of [spirit/assignment/system]. We revoke every claim and decree against [person/place] by the Blood. In Heaven's court this is registered. Amen."

For Loosing:
"In the name of Jesus, we loose heaven's flow: access, healing, restoration, and destiny. We declare gates open and blessings released. Seal it, O Lord. Amen."

For Sealing:
"Spirit of Judgment and Burning, seal this decree. By the Blood and by Your witness, make this lawful in Heaven and effective on earth. So it is, so it shall stand."

Closing: The Honour of Keys

Keys do not exalt those who hold them; they reveal who the Holder is. Use them to usher people into covenant, to restore what is lost, and to legislate mercy and justice. The Ekklesia that governs this way will find not only power but responsibility; not spectacle but stewardship; not noise but law.

When the Body sits rightly on its thrones and turns its keys with humility, heaven moves decisively and creation answers. This is the work of the court of Zion; serious, sober, and glorious.

CHAPTER 30

The Final Verdict: The Sabbath Government and the Eternal Rest

When all decrees are fulfilled and all thrones aligned, Heaven's final verdict resounds: REST.

Rest is not the cessation of work; it is the **completion of order**.

It is not silence; it is the harmony of every voice tuned to one frequency: **the will of God.**

The Sabbath is not a day; it is a *dimension of dominion*, where creation and Creator breathe as one.

1. The Sabbath as the Final Verdict

Every judgment of God moves toward reconciliation.
Every act of righteousness finds its conclusion in rest.
The Sabbath is the *verdict of divine justice;* peace established by judgment, order restored through righteousness.

Isaiah 32:17 declares,

> *"The work of righteousness shall be peace; and the effect of righteousness, quietness and assurance for ever."*

When righteousness reigns, warfare ceases.
When holiness governs, there is no rebellion left to fight.
The Sabbath is therefore not the end of history; it is the **beginning of eternal government**.

2. The Throne of Rest — Where Glory Dwells

Psalm 132:13–14

> *"For the LORD hath chosen Zion; He hath desired it for His habitation.*
> *This is My rest for ever: here will I dwell; for I have desired it."*

Zion is the Sabbath consciousness; the soul of creation brought back into alignment with the Spirit.
Here, the throne of the Lamb becomes the altar of the Spirit.
Here, the *Spirit of Judgment and Burning* completes His ministry, purifying the temple until it becomes God's rest.

Heaven does not rest because it is tired; it rests because **it is finished**.
When the fire has consumed all rebellion, the smoke clears, and only glory remains.

3. The Government of Peace

Isaiah 9:7 foretold it:

> *"Of the increase of His government and peace there shall be no end..."*

Peace is not the absence of conflict; it is the *presence of perfect government*.

The Sabbath Government is that realm where everything operates in rhythm with divine will.
Angels, saints, and creation move in synchronous worship, each performing their part without friction or rebellion.

This peace is judicial, not emotional.
It is the legal state of total reconciliation: Heaven's constitution fully enacted upon the earth.

4. The Spirit of Judgment and Burning — The Eternal Seal

Before rest, there must be fire.
Before habitation, there must be purification.
Isaiah 4:4 reveals the twin operation:

> *"When the Lord shall have washed away the filth of the daughters of Zion, and shall have purged the blood of Jerusalem... by the spirit of judgment and by the spirit of burning."*

The same Spirit who purifies is the One who dwells.
The fire that judged rebellion now becomes the light that governs.
This is the final mystery: **the Spirit of Burning becomes the Spirit of Rest.**
The flame does not depart; it simply stops consuming and starts illuminating.

The Sabbath throne is therefore a **fire-dwelling throne** — glory stabilised by holiness.

5. The Bride in Eternal Rest

Revelation 21–22 paints the closing vision:
The Bride is no longer preparing — she is reigning.
She no longer intercedes — she administrates.

She no longer waits for light — she becomes the light of nations.

The Sabbath is the marriage supper made permanent — worship enthroned as law.
The Spirit and the Bride say, *Come* — not as invitation alone, but as legislation.
They summon creation into rest.

> *"And the throne of God and of the Lamb shall be in it; and His servants shall serve Him: and they shall see His face" (Revelation 22:3–4).*

Service becomes sight.
Work becomes worship.
Government becomes glory.

6. The Completion of the Dominion Cycle

The sevenfold pattern of divine government now stands fulfilled:

1. **Creation** — The Word initiates.

2. **Law** — The Word defines.

3. **Judgment** — The Word tests.

4. **Redemption** — The Word heals.

5. **Glorification** — The Word ascends.

6. **Governance** — The Word reigns.

7. **Rest** — The Word abides.

This is the **Sabbath of Sabbaths;** the eternal equilibrium of God's administration, where every key has been turned, every seal opened, every throne occupied, and every sound harmonised into one eternal "Amen."

7. Zion — The Living Rest

Zion is not a location only; it is a *state of government in rest.*
It is where divine order and human obedience coexist without resistance.
The mind is Jerusalem, the heart is the temple, and the Spirit dwells as Sabbath.

Psalm 46:10 becomes literal:

> *"Be still, and know that I am God."*

Stillness is not passivity; it is dominion without effort.
It is the government that governs by being.
In Zion, existence itself is obedience.

8. The Eternal Law of Love

The final constitution of this government is Love, not as sentiment, but as structure.
Love is the alignment of will with will, purpose with purpose.
When every will in creation reflects the will of the Creator, the government is perfect, and the universe becomes worship.

The Sabbath is therefore the triumph of love over fear, harmony over rebellion, rest over striving.
It is the eternal "It is finished."

9. The Final Decree

> *"The Lord shall be King over all the earth: in that day shall there be one Lord, and His name one."*
> *— Zechariah 14:9*

The Court has adjourned.
The witnesses have testified.
The Blood has spoken.
The seals have been opened.
The verdict is REST.

Every throne finds its rhythm.
Every key returns to the Master's hand.
The fire that once judged now shines forever.
The Spirit of Judgment and Burning has become the Spirit of Dwelling and Glory.

10. The Sabbath Verdict — The Eternal Proclamation

Verdict of Heaven:
Peace established. Dominion complete. Glory eternal.
Let all creation enter the rest of the Lamb.

Decree of Zion:
"This is My rest for ever: here will I dwell; for I have desired it." — *Psalm 132:14*

Judgment of the Spirit:
"The fire shall dwell, and the glory shall govern."

Song of the Bride:
"Even so, come, Lord Jesus; dwell and reign within us, forever Sabbath."

The End of the Book — The Beginning of the Reign

The Sabbath Government is the consummation of all covenants,
The perfection of all justice,
The silence after the thunder,
The throne after the trial,
The *dwelling* of God with man —
Forever.

> *"And there shall be no more curse." — Revelation 22:3*
> *"For the LORD shall be unto thee an everlasting light,*
> *and thy God thy glory." — Isaiah 60:19*

7 Dimension Teaching Explained

I. Spiritology — The Throne of Rest

Rest is not the absence of motion but the completion of alignment.

In the Spirit, Sabbath is the frequency of divine stillness; the vibration of perfect order.

When Heaven's courts conclude their judgments, the Spirit releases one final sound: **"Peace, be still."**

This peace is the throne itself; the equilibrium of the divine Spirit seated within creation.

The Sabbath is the resting breath of God. It is when the Spirit stops contending and begins indwelling.

The Spirit no longer moves *upon* the waters (as in *Genesis 1:2*): He rests *within* the waters of the Word.

Every true saint becomes a living Sabbath, a dwelling place where God ceases from judicial warfare and begins eternal communion.

> *"And the work of righteousness shall be peace; and the effect of righteousness quietness and assurance for ever." — Isaiah 32:17*

II. Soulogy — The Mind as Zion, the Heart as Jerusalem

The soul is the inner court of the Sabbath government.

When the mind (Zion) is renewed, and the heart (Jerusalem)

purified, the divine government finds a throne within man.
This is not rest from labour, but rest from **double consciousness,** where the mind and heart are no longer divided by sin.

The soul at rest mirrors Heaven: thought and affection, intellect and emotion, will and worship — all reconciled in perfect unity. This is why *Psalm 132:13–14* speaks of Zion as *"My rest forever",* the inner mountain of divine indwelling.

When the soul enters Sabbath, anxiety dies, ambition bows, and desire becomes devotion.
The Sabbath is the sanctification of attention; the soul beholding only One Face.

III. Physiology — The Body as the Seat of Peace

Even the body partakes of this government.
The Sabbath anoints the body to cease from striving; every cell receives order from the Spirit.
The breath becomes prayer, the pulse becomes praise.
The temple of flesh becomes the living Ark, carrying the testimony of divine rest.

In resurrection, the glorified body of the saints will be Sabbath made visible; luminous flesh, breathing equilibrium, shining with the stillness of divine fire.

"For the earnest expectation of the creature waiteth for the manifestation of the sons of God." — Romans 8:19

The Sabbath is that manifestation, the transfiguration of creation through divine rest.

IV. Theology — The Lamb's Reign of Rest

The Sabbath is not merely a commandment; it is a **crown.**
The seventh day was not created for rest; it was begotten *in*

the rest.

When Christ declared, *"It is finished,"* the Sabbath throne was re-established in His blood.

Now the Lamb reigns not from labour but from rest; from the seat of eternal completion.

The theology of the Sabbath is the theology of fulfilled justice.

Every wound, every war, every word finds its consummation in the rest of the Lamb.

The cross was the gavel; resurrection was the verdict; Sabbath is the eternal decree.

V. Chronology — The 7000-Year Verdict

History is Heaven's courtroom transcript.

Six thousand years of labour, conflict, and decree — and then the seventh: the millennium of divine rest.

This is the Sabbath age; the thousand-year reign of Christ, where every kingdom submits to the Sabbath government.

Yet even beyond the millennium lies the eternal eighth day; the day that never ends, when rest becomes habitation, and time dissolves into eternity.

The Sabbath is therefore the hinge between time and timelessness, between judgment and glory.

VI. Typology — The Ark, the Temple, and the Throne

The Ark of the Covenant rested when the cloud rested; this was prophetic of the Sabbath Throne.

The Temple in Solomon's day was filled with glory, and "the priests could not stand to minister", that was the Sabbath's arrival in shadow form.

Now, in Christ, the true temple (His Body) has become the habitation of that glory.

The Sabbath is typified in the mercy seat; judgment beneath, glory above, rest in between.

It is the centre point where blood meets law, where mercy kisses truth.

Every type and shadow of Israel's worship finds its meaning in this one reality: **God has found rest in man.**

VII. Technology — The Divine Architecture of Eternal Rest

Heaven's government operates on spiritual technology: order, rhythm, and resonance.

The Sabbath is the frequency at which all divine systems stabilise.

Every key, every gate, every throne functions by rest. Without it, even revelation becomes rebellion.

When the saints align to Sabbath technology: Word, Breath, and Light, their decrees synchronise with Heaven's verdict.

This is how the Ekklesia legislates: not through noise, but through resonance.

Every "Amen" becomes a seal; every decree becomes light-law; every act of worship becomes governance.

Thus, the final architecture of creation is Sabbath; the unshakable kingdom, the unending peace.

The Lamb reigns, the Bride rests, the Spirit dwells.

The verdict is eternal: **Rest has triumphed.**

Closing Prophetic Seal

"For the LORD hath chosen Zion; He hath desired it for His habitation.
This is My rest for ever: here will I dwell; for I have desired it."
— Psalm 132:13–14

Here, the court of Heaven concludes.

The gavel strikes not in wrath but in worship.

The final word of judgment is **Rest.**

And the Sabbath becomes the everlasting government of God.

PRAYER

for Nationalisation into the
Kingdom of Heaven

Scriptural Foundation:

- *John 3:3 – "Jesus answered and said to him, 'Most assuredly, I say to you, unless one is born again, he cannot see the kingdom of God.'"*

- *Philippians 3:20 – "For our citizenship is in heaven, from which we also eagerly wait for the Savior, the Lord Jesus Christ."*

- *Ephesians 2:19 – "Now therefore you are no longer strangers and foreigners, but fellow citizens with the saints and members of the household of God."*

- *Colossians 1:13 – "He has delivered us from the power of darkness and conveyed us into the kingdom of the Son of His love."*

- *Romans 10:9 – "That if you confess with your mouth the Lord Jesus and believe in your heart that God has raised Him from the dead, you will be saved."*

Righteous Judge of Heaven and Earth,

I come before Your throne, the **throne of Grace** in **the Court of Heaven**, in the name of Jesus Christ, my Lord and Saviour. I stand by the power of His precious blood, which has **redeemed me** and **bought my salvation**. I come humbly and boldly, desiring to be **nationalised into the Kingdom of Heaven**—to become a **true citizen of Your heavenly realm**.

Father, Your Word declares in **John 3:3** that **unless one is born again**, they cannot see the Kingdom of God. Today, **I renounce any citizenship** I once held in this world and any **ties to the powers of darkness**. I acknowledge that I have been **transferred from the kingdom of darkness into the Kingdom of the Son** of Your love (*Colossians 1:13*). I declare that I am no longer a stranger or foreigner, but a **fellow citizen with the saints** and a member of the household of God (*Ephesians 2:19*).

Lord Jesus, I believe with all my heart that You are the **Son of the living God**, that You died for my sins and rose again to grant me eternal life (**Romans 10:9**). I now receive You as my **personal Savior, my Redeemer, the only Way, the Truth**, and **the Life**. You are the **Door to the Father's heart** and the only **path to salvation**. I do not want to **perish** with the world, but to **live eternally with You**.

At this moment, I [Your Full Name] solemnly, sincerely, and truthfully affirm my love, my seriousness, and my desire to follow You and serve You in **holiness and righteousness**. I pledge my full allegiance to You, O King of kings and Lord of lords. I give my loyalty to the third Heaven and honour its **rights and freedoms**. I desire to settle with You, **Lord Jesus**. I repent of the way I have **lived my life and of all my sins**. Take over **my heart and my destiny**. Save me, cleanse me, and change me.

I beseech that You **seal my heavenly citizenship today**. Let the record of **my new identity** be **registered in the Court of Heaven**. Write my name in the **Lamb's Book of Life**, and erase it from the **book of death and judgment**. Let every **legal claim the enemy** has over my past be **cancelled** and **rendered powerless by the blood of Jesus**.

Lord, I am ready to walk the path of **righteousness and holiness.** I cast all **my cares and all of myself upon You**, for You care for me and loved me and laid Your life as the Lamb slain from **the foundation of the world.** Let Your **will be done** in my life as it is in Heaven.

By Your blood, I now receive eternal life. I proclaim that I am a **new creature.** By the word of Your testimony, I am made free indeed. **Fill me and baptize me** with the **Holy Ghost and fire.** Thank You, Lord Jesus, for giving me the right and the power to become a child of God, born **not of flesh but of the Spirit,** according to **the new covenant sealed in Your blood.**

I believe **You died** for me, and on the **third day**, You rose again. You are now seated at the right hand of the **Father in glory**, and I receive You as the Lord of my life. Through You, I have **received grace, peace, forgiveness, and eternal inheritance.** I stand holy, blameless, and without fault before the **Court of Heaven** because of the **righteousness imputed to me through Your sacrifice.**

Now, I **declare that the power of sin, death, and Satan— including the grave**—has been **broken over my life.** I walk in the eternal victory of the Cross. From this day forward, I will never look back. Backward—never. Forward—forever.

Degree and Declare: I am a citizen of Heaven. I live for Your Kingdom. **I walk in Your authority and power.** I receive the **full inheritance of health, peace, righteousness, Wealth, and provision, even eternal life.**

In Jesus' mighty name, I pray.

Amen.

EPILOGUE

The Undisputed Heavyweight
Government (Deepened Version)

Now the scroll is sealed in fire, not with ink, but with Spirit.
The Word has taken its throne, and the Bride has taken her seat.
The Church has remembered her identity, not as an institution,
but as an incarnation.
She is Zion in motion; the voice of the Throne walking upon the
waters of time.

Every law of darkness has been overturned.
Every counterfeit dominion has been silenced.
The government of the Lamb now breathes through His Body;
not as doctrine, but as dominion; not as ritual, but as reign.

She speaks, and heaven responds.
She worships, and creation aligns.
She decrees, and time obeys.

The Church is not a weak assembly waiting for escape — she
is the ruling city descending from heaven, the bride adorned in
legislative light.
Her crown is not gold, but glory.
Her sceptre is not iron, but Spirit.
Her throne is not built of stone, but of hearts made perfect in
love.

Now the heavens declare her victory:
The Lamb has conquered through rest.

The Sabbath has become a kingdom.
The Spirit has found His habitation.

No gate of hell can contend with her; for she reigns not by strength, but by stillness.
She judges not by fear, but by flame.
She governs not by might, but by the breath of holiness.

She is the undefeated, undisputed, everlasting **Heavyweight Government of the Lamb** — the Body in whom God Himself sits enthroned.

> *"Of the increase of His government and peace there shall be no end, upon the throne of David, and upon His kingdom, to order it, and to establish it with judgment and with justice from henceforth even for ever."* — *Isaiah 9:7*

Selah — The Throne has returned to Zion.
The Sound has become Government.
The Rest has become Eternal.

AFTERWORD

When the Scroll Is Opened in You

The pages now lie behind you,
but the government they speak of stands before you.

This book was never meant to be information.
It was an activation.
A coronation.
A summons into the high places where the Lamb rules
and the saints sit beside Him as flames of judgment and rivers of
life.

You have not simply read about the Ekklesia: you have stepped
into her chambers, heard her sound, felt her fire, and witnessed
her ascension.

If something burned in you as you read,
that was not emotion.
That was calling.

If something aligned in you, that was not intellect.
That was the Spirit of Judgment and Burning reorganizing your
inner world to match the government of Zion.

The true Church is rising.
Not the church of brick and schedule.
The Church of throne and river.
The Church of key and seal.
The Church of oath and covenant.
The Church of rest and fire.

And now—you.

You are a witness of this government.
A vessel of this glory.
A governor in this Kingdom that cannot be shaken.

The nations will not be transformed by strategies alone,
but by saints who have become thrones.
By worshippers who have become judgments.
By intercessors who have become legislators.
By sons and daughters who no longer echo the world
but speak from the Council of Heaven.

This is your mantle now.

Carry it with humility.
Walk with the fear of the Lord.
Let every decree you release be soaked in love, and every verdict
burn with the wisdom from above.

And when you stand in the secret place, remember:
the Sabbath is your throne,
rest is your jurisdiction, and glory is your government.

The Lamb reigns.
The Ekklesia rises.
And you are part of the government
whose increase shall have no end.

Selah.

ACKNOWLEDGEMENT

To the One seated upon the Throne;
the Alpha of this message, the Omega of its revelation,
the Breath who carried every word,
the Fire who refined every page,
may this offering rise as incense before Your eternal counsel.

To the Holy Spirit;
the Architect of Zion,
the Voice behind the Voice,
the Teacher who unveils precept upon precept, line upon line,
until the Church remembers her crown.
Every insight in this work is simply Your whisper written down.

To Jesus Christ;
the Lamb enthroned,
the Governor of all ages,
the Sabbath of God made flesh.
Your reign is the rhythm of this book;
Your victory the substance of its hope.

To the Father;
the Ancient of Days,
whose government is peace,
whose rest is glory,
whose heart is Zion.
Thank You for choosing a people
through whom Heaven would speak again.

To those who walk with me in the journey of revelation; those

who pray, those who study,
those who hunger for the deep things of God —
your faith has been fuel,
your pursuit has been confirmation.
You are living stones in this rising house of fire.

To every reader;
called, chosen, awakened;
a king, a priest, a mountain of God in the earth.
May these pages not merely inform you but enthrone you.
May the Word you carry become government,
and the sound you release reshape nations.

This work is offered in humility and awe,
with gratitude for the grace to articulate
even a fragment of Heaven's design.
May the Lord Himself establish every truth written here,
and may His government increase in you
until the whole earth is clothed in light.

To the glory of the Lamb.
To the rise of Zion.
To the Ekklesia restored.

ABOUT THE AUTHOR

Anthony Mwangi — The Branch Seated In Zion

Anthony Mwangi carries a mandate forged in the quiet fire of encounter; a calling to decode the ancient patterns of Scripture and re-present the government of God for a generation standing at the threshold of divine transition. Operating as the BRANCH seated in Zion, he moves with a stewardship that blends prophetic insight, biblical precision, and a relentless pursuit of God's original order.

His work resonates with a single through-line: restoring the identity, authority, and priestly intelligence of the true Ekklesia. From the Sabbath as the signature of the Spirit to the stones of fire within the heavenly courtroom, Anthony builds frameworks that help believers step beyond religion and into divine functionality, the realm where sound becomes government and worship becomes strategy.

He writes as a witness, not a theorist; as a steward, not a performer. His teachings rise from the convergence of vision, Scripture, and Spirit-breathed revelation, weaving threads from Genesis to Revelation into cohesive architecture for the remnant church.

With a voice marked by clarity, urgency, and hope, he calls

God's people into maturity; to stand as priests, legislate as kings, and burn as witnesses of the Lamb's unending dominion. His life's work points to one outcome: a purified, awakened, governmental Church aligned with the throne of Christ, advancing heaven's agenda on earth with uncompromising fidelity.

Every page he writes carries the same pulse: the government of God is rising, and the sons and daughters of Zion must take their seat.

BOOKS BY THIS AUTHOR

Sabbath: The Name Of The Holy Spirit — God's Covenant Protocol For The Last Days: Yahweh, Yashua, Sabbath: The Signature Of God And The Rest Of The Spirit In The Last Days

This book unveils a groundbreaking revelation: the Sabbath is the Name, Seal, and Rest of the Holy Spirit, and the end-time Church cannot walk in covenant power without understanding this identity. Drawing from the 7-Dimensional Word of God, this work decodes the Sabbath as God's ancient–future protocol — the original sign of His presence, the governing code of His kingdom, and the prophetic mark that distinguishes His remnant in the last days.

You will discover how the Sabbath reveals God's hidden Name, aligns the mind with divine order, and positions the body as the dwelling place where the Spirit rests. From Eden's first seventh-day revelation to the sealed remnant of Revelation, this book demonstrates that to hallow the Sabbath is to hallow His Name, and that the restoration of Sabbath order is the restoration of God's government on earth.

Packed with visionary insights, prophetic typology, and a full blueprint for spiritual formation, this book equips believers to:

Understand the Sabbath as the signature identity of the Holy Spirit

Discern the covenant seal that separates truth from deception in the last days

Rebuild the altar of rest in the mind, heart, and body

Walk in the rhythm, protection, and judgment of God's kingdom order

Stand in Zion as those who have entered His Rest

This is not merely theology — it is kingdom strategy.
A call to return.
A summons to alignment.
A preparation for the remnant.

SABBATH: The Name of the Holy Spirit is your guide to reclaiming God's original covenant protocol, and stepping into the Rest that marks His people for the final generation.

The Issue Of The Horse: The Courtroom Indictment Against Easter, Christmas, And Modern Pagan Feasts

In a generation reshaped by convenience, tradition, and cultural drift, what if the greatest spiritual compromise is hiding in plain sight?

This book issues a bold, courtroom-level challenge to the most celebrated religious holidays: Easter, Christmas, and the modern feasts that carry the fingerprints of Babylon more than the signature of God.

Drawing from prophetic insight, forensic Scripture analysis, and the ancient protocols of the Holy Spirit, The Issue of the Horse unmasks the systems that led believers away from covenant identity and into ritual mixtures dressed as worship. It reveals how syncretism infiltrated the church, how altars were exchanged, and why heaven's court is calling for a return to purity.

This is not a rant. It's a verdict.
A clear, uncompromising case built line upon line—rooted in the King James Bible, reinforced by historical evidence, and charged with a future-focused mandate: to realign the body of Christ with the original statutes of the Spirit.

Readers will discover:

The prophetic meaning of "the horse" and how it exposes counterfeit worship

Why certain feasts carry a spiritual indictment

How the courtroom of heaven evaluates worship, sacrifice, and alignment

The clash between the Holy Spirit's Sabbath identity and modern religious tradition

The call of Zion for believers to return to covenant rest and Spirit-governed truth

This book is a wake-up call for believers, leaders, intercessors, and truth-seekers who know something is off but have lacked the language, evidence, and prophetic clarity to name it.

If you're ready to confront the mixture, reclaim ancient order, and stand in the firelight of truth,step into the courtroom.
The Spirit has issued a summons.
The verdict is unfolding.
And the remnant is rising.

The Armour Of Light: Unlocking The Mystery Of Divine Warfare

In the last days, the battlefield is no longer fought with swords and spears, but with light, truth, and the Spirit. The Armour of Light: Unlocking the Mystery of Divine Warfare is a prophetic unveiling of God's end-time strategy for His chosen remnant.

This masterpiece reveals the hidden dimensions of the Word of God and the power of the Holy Spirit as the true armour that clothes, protects, and empowers the believer. Through spiritology, soulogy, physiology, and theology, the mystery of warfare is unfolded—showing how the Sabbath is God's dwelling place, the Courtroom of Heaven is His battlefield, and the Bride is His warrior.

Drawing from ancient truths and prophetic revelations, Anthony Mwangi — the BRANCH seated in Zion — uncovers the role of man in God's eternal judgment, the secret of Christ's blood as the light of warfare, and the revelation of the 7-dimensional Word as the weapon that disarms the dragon, the beast, and the false prophet.

This book is not just a teaching, but a weapon in itself. It equips the end-time believer to stand clothed in fire, sealed by the Spirit, and ready to triumph in the last battle.

If you are called to be part of the remnant, this is your manual of divine warfare.

Authority Over The Seven Demonic Nations: A Spiritual Eviction Manual For Gatekeepers

Authority Over the Seven Demonic Nations: A Spiritual Eviction Manual for Gatekeepers is a prophetic warfare guide designed to expose and overthrow the ancient strongholds that still occupy the gates of your life, family, and inheritance.

Based on Joshua 3:10, this book reveals the spiritual identities behind the seven Canaanite nations—territorial powers that God commanded to be driven out. These are not just historical enemies; they are legal systems of defilement, fear, deception, generational bondage, pride, rejection, and dream manipulation.

Each nation is prophetically aligned with a ruling throne from the kingdom of darkness:

Canaanites – Lust / Defilement (Asmodeus)

Hittites – Wrath / Fear (Satan)

Hivites – Envy / Deception (Leviathan)

Perizzites – Sloth / Instability (Belphegor)

Girgashites – Greed / Ancestral Curses (Mammon)

Amorites – Pride / Domination (Lucifer)

Jebusites – Shame / Mockery (Beelzebub)

Through deep biblical revelation, courtroom language, and prophetic teaching, this manual will help you:

Identify the strongmen ruling over key gates in your life

Break legal rights and generational covenants that empower them

Rebuild spiritual altars and secure your inheritance

Activate your calling as a Gatekeeper in these last days

Pray elite-level courtroom decrees to dismantle demonic thrones

Whether you're a deliverance minister, prophetic intercessor, or believer hungry for spiritual authority, this book equips you to evict the enemy legally, spiritually, and permanently.

The thrones must fall. Your gates must be restored. Your territory must be cleansed.

Stars From The East (Irathiro)

The Scroll of Irathiro: The Rising Light from the East

From the snows of Mount Kenya to the throne of eternal fire, The Scroll of Irathiro unveils a prophetic revelation hidden for generations. This masterpiece carries the light of divine remembrance — a message to restore identity, awaken the remnant, and call nations back to covenant truth.

Through the 7-Dimensional Word of God and the Spirit's rhythm of revelation, the author unfolds mysteries connecting ancient prophecy, African identity, and the returning glory of Christ — the King whose hair is white as wool and whose eyes burn with eternal purpose.

Each chapter breathes with vision and fire: from the golden offerings of the Magi to the judgment of nations, from the altar of Zion to the rivers of counsel flowing from the throne. It is not merely a book — it is a scroll of destiny, written in light and sealed in blood.

Those who read will find themselves within the story of

restoration — called to stand as witnesses in the Court of Heaven, bearing the sign of the covenant and the song of the East.

Prophetic. Powerful. Undiluted truth.
This is not history retold — it is prophecy fulfilled.